Grapefruit League Road Trip

A GUIDE TO SPRING TRAINING IN FLORIDA

Ken Coleman with Dan Valenti

AAR

THE STEPHEN GREENE PRESS
LEXINGTON, MASSACHUSETTS

First published in 1988 by The Stephen Greene Press, Inc.
Published simultaneously in Canada by Penguin Books Canada Limited
Distributed by Viking Penguin Inc., 40 West 23rd Street, New York, NY 10010.

Maps drawn by Horvath & Cuthbertson

Library of Congress Cataloging-in-Publication Data

Coleman, Ken.
    Grapefruit league road trip.

    1. Baseball — Florida — Training — History.   I. Valenti,
Dan.   II. Title.
GV875.6.C65   1988   796.357′64′09759   87–21189
ISBN 0-8289-0652-1

Designed by Linda Koegel
Printed in the United States of America
by Haddon Craftsmen
set in Futura and Times Roman by AccuComp Typographers
Produced by Unicorn Production Services

Also by Ken Coleman and Dan Valenti
The Impossible Dream Remembered: The 1967 Red Sox
Diary of a Sportscaster

Also by Ken Coleman
So You Want to Be a Sportscaster

Also by Dan Valenti
Red Sox: A Reckoning
From Florida to Fenway
Cities Journey
December Sunlight

To my granddaughter Chelsea, to
my grandson Casey James: may
they both always live with the hope
that ''springs'' eternal within the
human breast.
—Ken Coleman

To the class of '65, Mt. Carmel
School, Pittsfield, Mass.; to Stanley
Kubrick; and to The Hill (and those
who made it possible).
—Dan Valenti

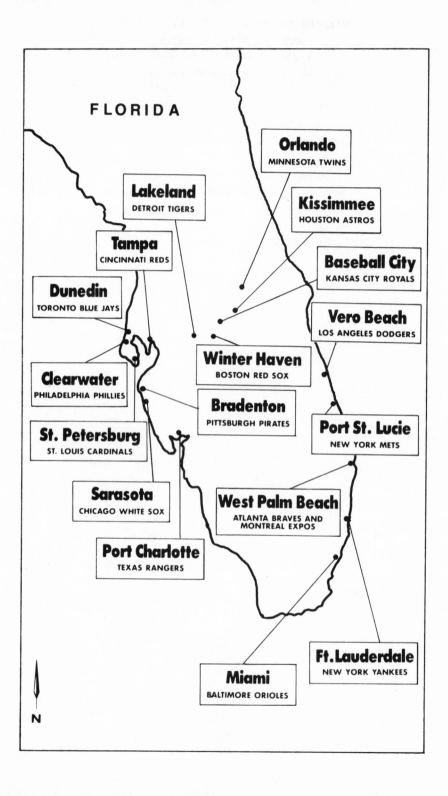

CONTENTS

Acknowledgments vi
Foreword vii

PART I TRAININ': A TIME TO DREAM   **1**

PART II   TRAVELIN': BEING THERE   **19**

Gulf Coast
Bradenton: Pittsburgh Pirates   23
Clearwater: Philadelphia Phillies   31
Dunedin: Toronto Blue Jays   38
Port Charlotte: Texas Rangers   45
St. Petersburg: St. Louis Cardinals 52
Sarasota: Chicago White Sox   61
Tampa: Cincinnati Reds   69

Central Florida
Baseball City: Kansas City Royals   77
Kissimmee: Houston Astros   85
Lakeland: Detroit Tigers   93
Orlando: Minnesota Twins   99
Winter Haven: Boston Red Sox   107

Atlantic Coast
Ft. Lauderdale: New York Yankees 114
Miami: Baltimore Orioles   122
Port St. Lucie: New York Mets   130
Vero Beach: Los Angeles Dodgers   137
West Palm Beach: Atlanta Braves
  and Montreal Expos   143

Before You Go 151

PART III   TRACIN': SCORECARDS   **157**

How To Keep Score 159

ACKNOWLEDGMENTS

Many people helped out with this book, especially in providing information on cities and teams. Our first thanks go to the chambers of commerce for each of the Florida towns covered inside. Next, we thank the public relations staffs of all the major league teams, who contributed so much.

Singling out particular people is always risky in a book like this, because so many helped . . . literally too many to mention. But we need to name a few for going above and beyond. Broadcaster Ernie Harwell of the Tigers; Steve Scruggs of the Winter Haven Chamber of Commerce; Susan Bloodworth of Boardwalk and Baseball's PR staff; Paula Baccoli for computer help; Jim Budka for St. Petersburg info; Boston Red Sox GM Lou Gorman; Tom Begner, our publisher, and Rickie Harvey, our publishette; Tom Hart for agenting; Literations; and finally, Ponce de León, who really made this book possible by discovering Florida.

FOREWORD

The best thing is that after you've pried your family out of the back of the plane, described your lost luggage to the airline, stood in the rental car line for longer than it takes to drive from Tampa to Vero Beach, and tolerated even longer lines at Disney World, they are human. These guys whom the NBC cameras equate to Schwarzeneggers and Redfords, whom Major League Baseball rules protect from signing autographs near your $14 regular season seat, whom their agents hold up and out for $1,300,000 (plus $25,000 for playing in 135 games, $125,000 for being named to the All-Star Game, and a single room on the road) turn out to be people.

You want Wade Boggs to pose with the wife and daughter, he poses. You tell Tim Teufel that you knew his neighbors back in Darien, and he asks about them. The day's routine is at 16 RPM, with time to share. They come wandering out of the clubhouses in ones and twos, standing around and chatting before the calisthenics begin at 10. They have mingling time during batting practice and after it, before and during the games; and as they come out of the games—to be replaced by guys with 50's and 60's on their backs—they still can stop and talk. In Dodgertown, which is what spring training is like if there is a spring training complex in heaven, there is Sandy Koufax, in his old uniform, throwing batting practice with fluid grace. In West Palm Beach, there is Henry Aaron with a 44 on his back, and in Ft. Lauderdale there are Whitey Ford and Mickey Mantle and Catfish Hunter, and perhaps the best thing about Winter Haven is that Ted Williams is there at 10 A.M., doesn't leave until 3:30, and will have his picture taken with every other person who 40 years earlier had pined for him.

And the crisp sounds of the bats and the balls. . . . You just have to keep in mind that spring training is the stretch before the six month marathon, and that Tim Corcoran—not Al Kaline, Carl Yastrzemski, or Dwight Evans—is the greatest slugger in Polk County's rich March history and that Mark Corey—not Don Mattingly or Eddie Murray—hit the longest home run in the history of Ft. Lauderdale Stadium, but it is personality that made Sam Horn a folk hero before he was even playing in New Britain and his personality came through in Chain O' Lakes Park.

It is baseball the way it is in Eliot Park on a Sunday morning, unofficial and sunburned, which is why spring training is as important as a Cardinal game on a Saturday afternoon at Wrigley or the entrance into Fenway of the Yankees on a June evening. To the junkie, it's even greater, for with a morning's walk around Dodgertown or Tigertown or the Winter Haven complex, one can take in players from the present, past, and future, all at a pace preserved from TV time-outs, mascots blocking your view, or megaboards orchestrating cheering. You may not be able to complete your scorecard by the time the managers have run 26 players in and out, but underlying it all is Chuck Tanner's statement that "the worst pressure in baseball is on a guy trying to make a team in spring training because his life's dreams are on the line."

Fifteen years ago, you could walk up the day of a game in most Florida ballparks and have your choice of all but about 1,000 seats. The cities outside of Miami were as bustling as Fitchburg. Eating was often done at your own risk. But spring training has become a vacational rite of spring. There are Disney World, Busch Gardens, and every kind of kiddie side trip east of California, and on the coasts there are beaches that make you wonder if anyone is in class back north. Games are sell-outs, hotels are booked solid, and you can't go a tenth of a mile without a full choice of soybeanburgers, beer gardens, and family restaurants with names like Steak 'N Cake. The parking lot outside Joker Marchant Stadium in Lakeland is 98 percent Michigan plates. Some nights Mario's in Winter Haven is booked solid with New Englanders, and Sabal's in Dunedin will be filled with Canadians the entire month of March.

It used to be that the first sign that winter was finally ending was the hollow, static-riveted sound of Ken Coleman or Ernie Harwell's voice announcing the Grapefruit League opener. Now, with all the lanes open from the north to Florida, baseball fans have made spring training theirs. Ken Coleman and Dan Valenti have presented a Florida guide for anyone who hasn't experienced these rites of spring — or, for those who have, a compendium of what you've missed. Once you've read the book, you cannot resist the trip, and once you've made the trip, you have to go back — for this is baseball simply for the fun of it.

— Peter Gammons

PART I

Trainin'
A TIME TO DREAM

THE PLAY'S THE THING

This is a book about spring training . . . about all the things that you will do in Florida when you go down to watch major league teams train. But before we tell you about each of the cities that host big-league ball, we'd like to tell you about spring training itself.

As far as the fan is concerned, spring training can be summed up in one word: "play." If it is nothing else, it is play. It is that great period of amnesty before the earnestness of the regular season, a time when the win-loss column is rendered meaningless. You can totally unwind and enjoy baseball in a way unlike any other. More on this later.

As a wise man once said: play so that later you may be serious. He wasn't speaking directly about spring training, but may just as well have been. Let us now enter this inviting land a little more deeply.

A PRODUCTIVE IDLENESS

Spring training is both a time and a place . . . a frame of mind and a thing to do. It is March in Florida . . . it is optimism and fun.

For you, the spring traveler, it is a time to be idle in a unique way, for this idleness is not unproductive. It is a soothing mental balm with which you bathe your winter-weary psyche. This massage of the spirit makes you come alive to simple pleasures all over again, pleasures such as the crack of horsehide against wood (what physician can measure the joy of hearing the first solid "CRACK" of the bat?) or the directness of a toasty sun baking newly cut outfield grass (what energy results from consuming such a recipe?).

The end result is rejuvenation at minimum, resurrection at maximum. You will return from your baseball vacation a warrior, a lion eager to take on the challenges and humdrum of your daily life. You will also be younger at heart, a creature put in touch with the child you once were.

Spring training is the Fountain of Youth that Ponce de León never found those hundreds of years ago in Florida. The roving Spaniard had the right geography, but the wrong time and the wrong game. It's baseball, Ponce, not exploration.

You don't think all this can happen? What can we say, except "check it out." When teams play baseball while it's yet winter in the rest of the country, crazy things will happen to you. No matter how much your vacation costs, you'll feel as though you're on the house's money. Baseball is a gift when it's Florida in March. It's your bonus, baby.

Remember that when you pay for those airline tickets, when you put that car rental on plastic, and when you hand over your $50 traveler's checks like so much Monopoly money to the hotel clerk, you aren't losing your money. You're gaining the sun.

BEGINNINGS

So how did it all begin for baseball and Florida? How did the two lovers meet, he the most reflective of all sports, she the alluring land of sunshine and warmth (and, if truth be told, of insects and Winnebagos)?

Long about the late 1880s, when baseball was establishing itself as the national pastime, an owner whose name has been long forgotten thought he'd get a jump on the competition by bringing his team south in March . . . far enough south so that they could play baseball. While rival teams were still shivering and out of shape "up north," his lads were getting into midseason form. Baseball and Florida haven't been the same since.

The game eventually led to the very redefinition of the flat, watery, warm peninsula. Besides all else that it was and would come to be, Florida had a further identity: it was where the big leagues played baseball when the North was still coping with snow and ice. This green land of sea-tickled coastal breezes and the sweet perfume of inland citrus had baseball when almost no one else did. Because of this, it had—and continues to hold—magic.

A TIME FOR FANS

Over the many years since the first Florida training camps, the experience of spring training—much like the state itself—has been defined and refined. Florida is now developed, built up. Condos proliferate. And try to travel more than an hour over the state's roadways without hitting the blight of Fast Food Boulevard—a pandemic stretch of seemingly endless burger/taco/chicken joints whose signs scream for your carbon monoxide–dulled attention: "This is the good stuff . . . billions and billions sold."

But the stadiums are for the most part clean, well-lit places. Highways are strategically placed. And airports meet the landscape upright, with enough service to enable you literally to get out of winter and end up under a hot ballpark sun in a matter of hours, on a day of your choosing. It is a world of miracles, indeed. And so you depart. The silver bird wings you, the iron horse rails you (there is no lyrical term for a bus) to the South.

You arrive. You go to a spring training camp. What do you find?

Make no mistake. Spring training isn't for the players. It's for the fans, which is to your advantage. Most players agree they don't need six weeks to get into playing shape. Today's players, in fact, are rarely out of shape. With so much money on the line (a 1988 average salary of more than $400,000 a year), conditioning is a year-round pursuit. Their bodies are their jobs. Their worry is more about getting *out* of shape during spring training.

"When the exhibition games begin, there's too much time for sitting and standing around. The only real workout I get is following games, when I do windsprints," says three-time National League MVP winner Mike Schmidt of the Phillies. "Look at them," he continues, pointing to a group of players standing and sitting in the outfield. "They're telling stories and killing grass. A lot of them aren't in good enough shape to play any other sport."

It wasn't always like this. In the fifties, for example, the minimum wage in baseball was $7500, and about half the players made the minimum. In the off-season, they had to work someplace to make ends meet. When spring training came around, it meant hard work: several weeks to get into a semblance of playing shape.

Hang around a spring training camp after the third or fourth week, and just about everyone on the team—except the workaholics, the rookies, and an occasional left-handed pitcher—is bored.

As Stan Musial used to say, he didn't need all of spring training to get ready for the season. All he needed was "ten days to get the blisters on my hands and have the blisters turn to calluses."

Teams are itching to get the season started. Teams, that is; not the tourists.

The tourists want it to last and last. And why not? They are removed from their lives of daily care. They're *off* the job. They live in hotels where the beds make themselves and the towels are invisibly changed. There is no job to go to. There are no meals to cook. There are few responsibilities. There are only Florida and baseball . . . both to enjoy.

Florida and the Traveler engage in a pretty one-sided dialogue:

FLORIDA: Give me your sick of winter, your huddled masses in need of sun. Send me your tired who need the relaxing mathematics of box scores to games that are exempt from pressure. Give me your weary. I will give you home runs. Abandon your worries. I will give you infields. TRAVELER: Gladly. Take of me my all.

To repeat our question: what do you find in Florida when it hosts major league baseball?

The detailed and specific answers to this question make up almost the whole of Part II of this book. But for now, let's answer it in a different way.

NOTHING AND EVERYTHING

What can you expect of spring training? We don't want to go too far here for fear of planting preconceptions that may affect your openness to the baseball adventure that awaits you and your family. So we tell you, in once sense, expect nothing.

That's right, nothing. Only by avoiding preconceptions, and letting go of a few of your expectations, can you fully open up to new experiences or experience familiar ones anew. Dropping your ideas of how things *should* be enables you to see them as they actually are. That can be fun, and there is much to see in Florida during March. Because there is so much to see, there is, in fact, much to expect.

Do we contradict ourselves? Not really, for we're talking about spring training, and this type of baseball—as Walt Whitman said of himself—"contains multitudes." So what can you expect?

You can expect the exhilaration of simply being around a hot, sunny ballpark when you'd normally be somewhere like Buffalo or Scranton, dealing with gritty ice, cutting winds, and icy cold. There's something so incredibly delightful about this that you'll actually feel younger. Cares will evaporate. Wrinkles will disappear. The superpowers will unilaterally and coincidentally disarm, ushering in a millenium of world peace. You will walk with a bounce in your step just short of dancing. You won't believe how much fun the game of baseball can be. You'll also wear a smug smile when you read about the latest snowfall back home.

You can expect the surprise of seeing your favorite ball players up close, touchable close, warts-and-all close. You can enjoy talking with them . . . questions, comments, all sorts of banter. Players will be less the idols that they appear to be on TV or in the papers, or that you make them out to be from the concrete vastness of most of today's major league stadiums. Rather, they will appear more like what they are — can you believe it? — more like actual, living, breathing, friendly and sometimes grouchy human beings. They'll welcome you, and they'll snub you. This affects fans in different ways; it's safe to say your perceptions of baseball will change.

You can expect to spend more than you should but less than you'd like on souvenirs: T-shirts, sweatshirts, wristbands, yearbooks, buttons, pennants, posters, books, media guides, place mats, postcards, trading cards, baby bibs, mugs, hats, knickknacks, wall hangings, bumper stickers, and the like.

You can expect the cheery feeling that comes from watching big-league baseball in what are essentially minor league ballparks. It's the best of both worlds in that sense. Florida parks have a certain quaint aspect to them. You're close to the action. You can usually see everything well. There's a closeness to the players that breeds a comfortable feeling of intimacy. Players in the bull pen are near the fans, and conversations ensue. This stuff is next to impossible in a modern major league park, whose sterile vastness creates an impenetrable barrier between audience and performer.

You can expect to see players in training. This sounds obvious, but what it means is that you may see some ragged ball in the exhibition games. A manager likes to look at new faces and new lineups that normally he wouldn't use in the regular season. Early in the exhibition season, you'll see a lot of rookies and marginal players. The longer the camp goes on, the more you'll see of a team's regular lineup. A manager also will manage differently in exhibitions. For example, he might leave a struggling pitcher in the game just so he can get his work in. Remember, the win-loss record of spring training is next to meaningless.

You can expect veteran players, especially pitchers, to pace themselves. Nolan Ryan is a perfect example. The first couple of times he pitches in an exhibition game, he throws at half or three-quarters speed. All he wants to do is get a feeling about being on the mound and looking at live competition. There's no way he will throw hard early. Tom Seaver was like this. Thus, the early spring stat lines also are unimportant.

So be patient with the baseball you see. Ralph Houk would never make any evaluations or judgments about pitchers until they had pitched three times. Veterans will be careful not to overextend themselves too early. Of course, with a rookie, it's a totally different situation. He has to impress fast, immediately, and he will—should—go as hard as he can as early as he can. Incidentally, that's why young players will sometimes play winter ball: so they can arrive in camp, ready to go full tilt.

Keep in mind, however, that while the scores don't matter, there's still an edge of tension in camp. Be it the unknown rookie trying to make the club or the marginal veteran trying to squeeze out one more year, management is always watching . . . every pitch, every at bat.

One more thing: you'll notice a certain laxness in the rules of the game. For example, if a spring game is tied after nine innings, the teams may, by mutual agreement, end the game there.

You'll see some weird things, such as extra guys on the field. When the regulars are taken out of the game, they'll usually get in their running on the warning track, behind the outfielders, while the game is in progress. When you see it happen, don't yell to the umpire: "Hey, get those guys off the field."

HOT TIPS

Now a couple of quick tips. We'll give you a whole lot more in Part II, but for now, these will come in handy.

If you intend to come down to spring training for a couple of weeks or more, the best time to arrive is before the start of the exhibition games. Before the games begin (usually around March 7), teams hold daily workouts and practice sessions. They are free and great fun. You'll see all sorts of fielding and baserunning drills and get a chance to witness the players at work, in effect, behind the scenes.

The workouts are informal, with a good deal of joking and horseplay . . . and that's their beauty. But remember, unlike games workouts begin early, usually at 10:00 A.M. If you show up at 1:00 in the afternoon, almost all the activity will be over.

As for the games, allow yourself *plenty* of time to get to the park. The traffic and crowds will likely be fierce near game time. Show up early and leave a little later; you'll save yourself a lot of grief sitting around in a backed-up parking lot.

An important thing to remember, especially your first day or two in Florida, is to watch yourself in regard to the sun. The southern sun is intense, hotter than you'll notice on that first day. The temptation is to soak up as much of "ol' sol" as quickly as you can on your largely uncovered body. This can be dangerous. You risk bad sunburn and even hospitalization from overexposure. So don't get too much sun on the first day or two. Also, use plenty of sunscreen. Wear a cap and long sleeves and increase your exposure gradually. Better yet, get a genuine store-bought artificial tan before you even get to Florida. Then you can get the sun off your mind entirely. It won't be so much of an obsession, and as such, you can enjoy yourself a whole lot more.

Another weather note. Though you'll get hot weather in March, you can also get some iffy days: wind, rain, and some chill, especially at night. Even on sunny days, if the wind is blowing and the temperature is in the sixties, and you're sitting in the shady part of the stands, you will be uncomfortable if you don't have a jacket. So it's always better to bring that extra piece of apparel. Better to be safe than cold.

If you're interested in following your favorite team in the papers, remember that your hometown paper may not be available in Florida. If it is, it's most likely to go at an unhealthy premium (a 25-cent paper for 75 cents). No sweat. The local media in each of the Florida towns usually will have in-depth coverage. For them, this is the big-league season, and for the most part, they give it big-league coverage. They'll cover the camps every day, until the teams head north. Also, *USA Today* runs items from each of the training camps every day.

A TIMELESS TIME

Now it's time to continue our look at spring training, in all its clarity and haze, through the sharpness of a bright, cloudless day; through the mist of a steamy shower; through the quiet action of the morning sun, lifting off the grass's dew drops; through our heart's colorings and our mind's eye.

If life begins on opening day, as Thomas Boswell asserts, then its conception begins in spring training, when teams come together in their winter-hatched aspirations. The February/March sun at first seems incongruous, especially in the early days of camp. In these first days, the beat, or mood, of the camp begins to take shape. Almost without exception, the character of a spring camp proceeds from hope.

If a ball club is ever to dream, as its fans surely will, it must do so in the spring, for that's the only time it can do so with impunity. Spring training is that period of baseball between its image and reality. All teams are undefeated, all are tied for first place, and there is no evidence whatsoever to dispute anyone's claim to upcoming greatness.

Spring training is the timeless time that intervenes between the first dream of a pennant and the first pitch on opening day, when all bets are off, everything is for keeps, and no prisoners are taken. Once the season begins, reality takes over and most decidedly puts baseball back in time . . . not the time of a clock, but the time imposed by a relentless 162-game schedule. With each at bat, with each inning, with each win or loss of the regular season, a case is being built—an argument being made—for or against a team's spring dreaming.

THE LAST IS FIRST

Let's look into this phenomenon more closely, because understanding this difference between training camp and the regular season is crucial to the maximum appreciation of—to getting the most from—your trip to Florida.

Spring training gives credence to a piece of Biblical wisdom that says "The last shall be first." For the first and last are really on equal footing in the spring. The last shall be first because the last *is* first. As we said, who can prove otherwise?

The grapefruit league records mean little, and every manager can excuse a poor showing simply by saying that when opening day gets here "We'll be OK." This will appease the die-hard fans and temporarily silence the critics.

In that first week of March, the new baseball season is as innocent and treasured as a newborn baby. It is cuddled in the arms of the fans, who coax it into saying its first halting words. These words are mostly gibberish, such things as "We're only two or three players away from a pennant," or "We hope to be fighting all the way this year," or something about this being a "rebuilding" year ("rebuilding": baseball's euphemism to describe the actions of losing teams).

Another favorite piece of child babble involves the Phenom. The Phenom is that raw kid who does something outlandish to impress both the manager and the media ("hardest ball I ever saw hit"). You hear such comments as "This kid can't miss. He's another Mantle."

For the fans, this is almost too good to be true. They are like all parents with a newborn: their joy will spare no rosy outlook. No possibility can seem too remote. Even those who won't admit it publicly secretly hold hope (hope, in fact, is implicit in the definition of a "fan").

So you can say anything you want in the spring. You can claim improvement. You can offer tantalizing and enigmatic claims of "contention." You may even claim a championship, because miracles happen just enough to justify this madness. To wit the 1914 Boston Braves, the 1967 Boston Red Sox, or the 1969 New York Mets. You will skip through the days of spring training to the background strains of Pan's lyrical flute.

Then the calendar sheds its page from March to April like some alluring dancer doing a strip tease. You are all excited about opening day. You cannot contain your passion . . . until your team's first *real* loss. Then you notice the music has changed. The pastoral flute has given way to the first four notes of Beethoven's Fifth: destiny knocks on the door. Each pitch means something now.

It is later than you think.

Copernicus lost us in space. Darwin lost us in time. Freud lost us in ourselves. Opening day loses us in the reality of the team we call our own.

The regular season starts, and for most teams, the cream sours and sinks to the bottom. It's here that another piece of wisdom takes over—this uttered by Leo Durocher about two thousand years after "The last shall be first." Now, it's "Nice guys finish last."

The dream is over, bud. It got the bum's rush when the training camps closed their doors. What took the place of the reverie? Baseball Darwinism.

On and after opening day, only the fit will survive. Pale-skinned statisticians sit before the pulsing green glow of computer screens, recording all the millions of bits and bytes contained in the abrupt but all-inclusive typography of "W's" and "L's." The baseball record has permanence, such that, one hundred years later, someone will be able to (shudder) look it up.

In short, on and after opening day, the time for excuses and gibberish ends. So does the luxury of hiding in a hope. Sentences must make sense. They must be direct and to the point as they take on the challenge of explaining why your team is twelve games out.

Once the season begins, a team's foundation of hope comes under scrutiny. As certain as three strikes is an out (Mickey Owen excluded), some teams begin to lose hope. For some, dreams become walking nightmares. It must be true that when you find yourself in last place in August, you wish it could be spring all over again . . . the spring just passed, the spring to come. Any spring.

Fans know this hard truth much better than players, for it is left to fans to stay with a team the longest. A player may be with a team for ten years, and we say he's had a long career. A fan, however, often has put in that much time while still in his or her midteens. Fans are usually in it for life (again, this is another thing implicit in the definition of "fan").

That's why spring training should mean so much to them, and why they cheat only themselves if it doesn't. In the spring, they are exempt from the utter seriousness of living and dying with their team and can enjoy baseball—and most everything else—with the pressure off; to borrow from football: instead of third and 26 from your own 12, it's first and goal from the 1.

You should show up for spring workouts and games ready to have fun, to sit back in the sun. Buy a couple of hot dogs, some peanuts, maybe some soda or beer. Nothing more. What inspections you do of your team should be performed not like a juror but more like a member of the reviewing stand in your hometown Fourth of July parade.

The troops may look slightly out of step, and the notes to "Seventy-six Trombones" may sound a little flat. But you and your fellow reviewers smile at the mistakes, patting the band members on the head. "A" for effort. Throw to the right base. Learn that pickoff move. Hit the cutoff man. If not today, then tomorrow. No problem.

In spring, we seem to have no trouble remembering the nature of an error:

> And in the days before Confucius became a philosopher and a wise man, he was a baseball manager. Once, in a spring training game, his rookie shortstop made three errors, the last of which allowed the winning run to score. After the game, Confucius said nothing to the distraught young man. The following day, however, Confucius went up to the disconsolate shortstop and said, "Being foolish yesterday makes it easier to be wiser today."

WHAT IS THIS SPRING?

Spring training admits no losers, no .210 hitters, no earned run averages above four, no mistakes. No matter what, at the end of camp, all columns on the stat sheet click over like an odometer changing from all nines to all zeroes at a fun journey's end—from the uneven, jumbled numbers of results to the well-rounded form of zeroes. Baseball's perfect symmetry.

Spring training is repetition . . . endless batting, running, and fielding drills. Interminable interviews. Six weeks of living in a motel room. Six weeks of running out of places to eat. This repetition breeds a feeling of security in baseball people and creates in them a feeling of normality. That's it. All feels "normal" in the spring ("normal": one of those words like "reality" that, as writer Vladimir Nabakov pointed out in his masterwork *Lolita*, means nothing without quotes).

Spring training is the one and only time when all teams can participate equally in baseball. Everyone has similarly justified visions of sugarplum fairies and pennants dancing in the head. Democracy at work.

The action of spring is baseball; the talk, baseball. Both are refreshingly pure and simple. For baseball is a subtle game, and spring training is its most uncomplicated moment. As a fan, it will be enough that baseball is being played. If your team wins, so much the better. But such a win is a bonus, added value.

A truism about baseball fans: they are impatient over the pitch, long suffering over the at bat; critical during the inning, understanding over the game; doubtful for the game, sympathetic for the season; cynical for a season, loyal for a lifetime.

In the long run, they forgive, but not always for the specific moment. This makes spring training even more special.

Because the grapefruit season is so brief and because, when camp breaks, all results are wiped out as surely as dear Custer on those bluffy South Dakota hills a few million years ago, everyone loves to forgive everything.

The sun is warm, the air smells of sea mist, oranges, and coconut oil. Fans love to forgive because they *can* forgive. We have, in short, baseball's equivalent to that wonderful state called peace of mind.

Traveler and fan, your money is well spent when spent on such therapy.

TENSION AND TYPES

Earlier, we mentioned the edge of tension in a spring training camp. Let's examine this, for fans may not be all that aware of this element.

Remember, there are guys fighting for jobs and working hard for uncertain futures. When a rookie pitcher takes the mound for his first appearance of the spring or a thirty-seven-year-old veteran finally gets an at bat late in the game as a pinch hitter, don't speak to them of spring's myth or magic. Recite not the fair poetry of sun-dabbled days and carefree baseball.

Talk, maybe, of sleepless nights, food that won't stay down, or the fear of being cut. Talk to them of the possibility of being sent down to the minors. Talk, perhaps, of the bus rides, the inadequate meal money, the dimly lit parks with empty seats if they don't somehow make the team. Talk, if you feel up to it, of outright release ("Oh, that magic feeling. Nowhere to go . . ."").

Florida's camps house four kinds of players. Knowing the types will help you better understand what spring training is all about.

First, there are a team's starters and stars. No sweat here, in this high-rent district of multiyear, guaranteed, big-buck contracts. Next are the solid players who—by virtue of their position, experience, skills, or versatility—are sure of making the team. These are followed by rookies and unknowns who know in their hearts they don't have a chance, at least not this year. Shed no tears yet.

Finally, there are the in-betweeners, those ball players on the dividing line between success and failure, the "maybe-they-will, maybe-they-won't" group. This last group, by far, has it the toughest. This bunch consists of young players with fast-dying chances and veterans who may have lost it. For them, every inning, every at bat is the bottom of the ninth in a tie game, two outs, bases loaded.

A case in point.

Several years ago, spring training 1981 to be exact, Joe Rudi, then thirty-four, was in Winter Haven trying to make the Red Sox roster. Some openly wondered in camp if Rudi's better days were behind him and if he were washed up. Joe must have known the same doubts, and he pushed himself ruthlessly, despite nagging leg injuries. In the same camp that year was Roger LaFrancois, an anonymous catcher with the odds stacked against him higher than a winter's supply of firewood piled outside a home in the Maine woods.

One day, both voluntarily took extra batting practice while the rest of the team was enjoying a day off. Supervising the session? None other than Ted Williams. Let's drop in. To repeat: this happened on a day off. These guys should have been relaxing. Instead, driven on by desperation, they voluntarily entered the batting cage and threw away the key.

You are there.

The workout has been going on for about an hour and a half in eighty-four-degree weather. Rudi takes fifty swings in the cage against the B.P. serves of minor league coach Rac Slider, then gives way to LaFrancois. Williams watches silently. As the rookie steps in and hacks away from the left side (with much less precision and purpose than Rudi), Williams directs his eyes on him like laser beams.

"Now ya see what you're doing with your hands, Rog?" Ted booms. "What are you doing?"

"I'm dropping them too much," Roger replies.

"Yeah, just what we talked about the other day."

LaFrancois is aware of the mistake, and that pleases Williams. He steps back in the box. This time, he concentrates on proper hand position. Slider throws. LaFrancois turns on the pitch and rifles it out to right center. He stings the next pitch down the right field line.

"Now look at that," Williams shouts excitedly to him. "You look at those hands now!" he says.

More hacks for Roger, then Rudi bats again, cracking line drives all over the outfield. As he follows through with his swing, he grimaces in pain from a severe leg muscle pull. Unconsciously favoring the leg, he turns his head slightly after each swing. So slightly, in fact, that it's unnoticeable . . . except to Williams, who picks it up and points it out for the unseeing (let he who has eyes see).

"Joe, let me ask you a question. Why are you dropping your head back at the end of your swing?" Rudi says he was unaware of the movement. "Guess it's the leg." He steps back in, corrects, and sends the ball even farther, harder.

When Rudi is done, Williams talks with him.

"Joe, you've got a damn good swing. You don't ever have to worry about that. But, jeez, don't give them pitchers any more advantage than they already have. A pitcher is the dumbest son of a bitch in the ballpark. A pitcher will scratch his ass and never know how he got you out. The truth is, they get batters out because the hitters help them too much. That's why when you start moving your head or holding your hands in the wrong place, you're taking the bread and butter right out of your own mouth."

Ted takes an imaginary bat in his hands and swings viciously — but purposefully — at an imaginary pitch. After Ted leaves, both veteran and rookie, knowing what's at stake, resume their workout. They are there for another ninety minutes. The park is near empty. The crack of the bat echoes lonely in the Florida air. Each noise may be an encouragement — or an indictment. The player can never be sure.

Rudi made the team that year and hit .180. Soon after, he was out of baseball. LaFrancois was cut, his career (five at bats in '82) fading out like the spiral grooves that end a record that never makes the charts.

Besides the four types of players, be aware of the coaches, those slow-moving men with time-wizened faces. They have seen it all before. Everything.

For them more than anyone, spring training is renewal, the chance to share once again the world of young men. Their eyes are deep as wells as they look at young players. They see themselves, and aren't they right?

Doesn't a good coach, by imparting his knowledge of baseball, offer nothing less than a part of himself, a part that can later find expression through the career of a young man? That's why good advice is eternal and why good coaching is selfless. It gives of itself so that wisdom may live through the play of another. When Roger Clemens goes to the mound or Don Mattingly steps up to the plate, their coaches go with them. When one gives of the self in this way, he doesn't lose part of himself. He gains a larger, less selfish, identity.

But, as we know, not all advice leads to success. Players fail. Yet even this bitter personal letdown gets swallowed whole by the game itself.

When a player fails to make it in baseball, as most minor leaguers will, the loss is momentary. For each failure there are ten, twenty, or more kids waiting for a chance to fill the uniform. In such a game, individual failure matters little. The empty spot on the roster will be filled tomorrow, or next year, until time and whatever forces destiny has to command produce a Babe Ruth, a Ted Williams, or a Willie Mays.

Coaches know this. They know it without necessarily knowing they know. They have seen it all. Everything.

MEMORIES ARE MADE OF THESE

Now a word in general about the travels that await you. We will get very detailed in Part II.

In Florida you will be met by contrast: the forest-lined beauty of lonely state roads and the motorway madness of an emptying stadium parking lot. The glare and blare of Disney World and the reflections of a sunset on a quiet inland backwater. The gourmet-class cuisine of a world-class restaurant and a ballpark hot dog. The reverie of the Ft. Lauderdale Strip and the sleepy eyes of Yeehaw Junction. The soft white sands of Clearwater Beach and the hard, black, hot tar of a shopping mall parking lot. The awestruck eyes of a kid getting an autograph and the quiet gaze of a senior citizen watching his four thousandth game. Alligators sunning by a lake and fire ants buzzing like animated exclamation points. The billboard-covered outfield walls of Tinker Field in Orlando and the outfield with *no* fences at Dodgerland in Vero Beach. Batting cages and bull pens. The paving of flesh with mercurial oils and the ginger covering of the same flesh later glowing lobster red. The popular Phenom and the forgotten veteran. The spacious green of the outfield and the pinching brown of the batter's box. Nineteen eighty-eight Jaguars with vanity plates and 1976 Gremlins with cracked windshields. The strip joints on Orange Blossom Trail outside Orlando and the myriad churches of the Bible Belt. A pitcher in the bull pen chatting with a fan in the grandstands and a superstar snubbing the press. The tradition-steeped town of Sarasota, with decades of spring training memories, and the gleaming newness of the Mets camp in Port St. Lucie.

When you are not watching baseball, you will be met by variety: college kids in jams. Palm trees. Sailboats. Blue water. Over-priced souvenirs. Corny postcards that you can't help but buy so you can send them back home as a kind of elbow in the ribs ("You are up there; I am down here. . . . You are chiseling ice off your windshield; I am downing a cool one poolside"). Fishing. The Inveraray Golf Classic in Lauderhill. The Sanibel Island Shell Fair. The Weeki Wachee Springs Mermaid Show. The Snake-a-Torium on U.S. 98 in Panama City Beach. The Salvador Dali Museum in St. Petersburg. The Kennedy Space Center. The Miami Wax Museum. Retirees (more than 2 million over age sixty out of a state population of 9 million). The Cugat rhythms of a Latino dance band. Young women in afterthought bikinis. The speaking silence of Saint Leo Abbey on Highway 52, thirty miles north-west of Lakeland. The Kissimmee Livestock Market. The dazzling plants of Cypress Gardens. And on and on.

TESTING A DREAM

So your visit to the Land of Spring Baseball goes. Your vacation's grasp taking you beyond the reach of worry. The white, red-stitched baseballs finding their way into the hands of your consciousness. A foul-ball souvenir put on the mantel of the soul's fireplace, that place where burns the spark of what and who you are.

Before you came down to Florida, the fire was just a few spent embers glowing amid the gray ashes of routine, daily life. Now you are glowing with a warmth that comes from a contented intensity. An intense con-tentedness. It is all special, you see, this thing called spring training.

PART II

Travelin'
BEING THERE

HOW TO USE PART II

This part contains information on each of the Florida cities that hosts major league baseball during spring training. Cities are presented alphabetically within one of three geographical regions: the Gulf Coast, Central Florida, and the Atlantic Coast. Each city functions, in effect, as a separate chapter.

Sometimes within our city "chapters," we refer you to the chamber of commerce for more information. We should point out that the address and phone number of each local chamber is presented at the end of each chapter. The chamber can be one of your most valuable resources when you're traveling. They have the information and the resources to help you with almost every aspect of your trip. Learn to use this resource. In fact, it would be wise to contact the chamber about a month before you leave. They will send you information that, along with this book, will well equip you for your journey.

In each of the city chapters, we present information on the team and its facilities, the area itself, the major attractions, and suggestions on where to stay and eat. Our lists of accommodations, restaurants, and attractions are not recommendations, but rather possibilities for you to check out. It's always a good idea to shop around. Find out about more than one place before making a decision.

Bradenton

PITTSBURGH PIRATES

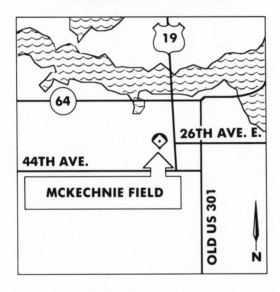

THE TEAM

The Pirates have made their winter home in Bradenton since 1969. The Bucs run their camp from a headquarters known as Pirate City. They play their exhibition games at McKechnie Field.

TEAM HOTEL   None. Players and team executives who do not make private arrangements for condos or apartments are housed at Pirate City.

PIRATE CITY   A forty-nine-acre baseball complex, Pirate City is used virtually year round by the Pirates organization. From the middle of February to the first week of April, the major league team trains there. The Pirates minor league operation uses the site from the middle of March to early May. From the middle of June to early September, the site is home of the Bradenton Pirates of the Gulf Coast League for rookies. From late September to late November, the facility is used by clubs in the autumn Instructional League.

The complex has living quarters for well over 200 ball players. Facilities include a huge dining room with kitchen, a laundry, a staff lounge, conference rooms, a players' lounge, offices for club executives, and accommodations for the media.

Practice sessions are held daily on four full-size playing fields surrounding an observation tower. From the tower, visitors can watch the Pirates practice on all four fields. The diamonds are well maintained, with a computer-controlled sprinkling system using well water. Running tracks, sliding pits, night lighting, and the usual assortment of batting cages complete the facilities.

The forty-man roster of the major league Pirates conducts workouts at Pirate City until the first week of March, usually around March 5 or 6.

Address and Phone   Pirate City, P.O. Box 1359, 1701 Roberto Clemente Memorial Drive, Bradenton 33505; (813) 747-3031.

MCKECHNIE FIELD   Sometime near the end of the first week of March, the major league Pirates switch workouts and camp to McKechnie Field, across town. Workouts are held from 10:00 A.M. to 1:30 P.M. Workouts are open to the public without charge.

The Pirates typically play about sixteen exhibition games at McKechnie Field, where ticket prices run $3 for general admission ($1 for kids), $4 for reserved seats, and $5 for box seats. Ticket office hours are 9:00 A.M. to 4:00 P.M. Monday through Friday. Game time is at 1:30 P.M.

Season tickets for spring training games go on sale in the third week of January. Individual game tickets are available in the second week of February. For box seats, season tickets are $70 each. Reserved seats cost $56.

Rickety McKechnie Field has a charm that evokes baseball in its simpler, more pastoral time. Attendants park cars in nearby grassy fields, and the feeling is not so much like major league baseball but more like a county fair. The wooden stands have seen their share of baseball history. Before the Pirates, McKechnie hosted the Braves of Boston and Milwaukee, and before that, the Gas House Gang of the St. Louis Cardinals. Dizzy Dean even owned a gas station in town. **Address and Phone** McKechnie Field, 17th Avenue W. and 9th Street W., Bradenton 33505. Ticket office: (813) 748-4610. Press box: (813) 746-6477.

THE AREA

Manatee County, which contains Bradenton, boasts twenty miles of Florida's best beaches, an array of water sports, light-hearted special events, many historical sites, fresh seafood dining pleasures, close proximity to theater and concerts, plus a selection of accommodations ranging in price from an average of $40 to $100 per night.

BEDDING DOWN Unlike some island resort areas, individuals and families visiting the Manatee County area can find accommodations to fit both budget and life-style. Here are a few possibilities:

Bahia Court 1905 Cortez Road W., Bradenton 34202; (813) 755-2188. 10 rooms and efficiencies, nightly/weekly rates.

Baxters Motel 3225 14th Street W., Bradenton 33505; (813) 746-6448. Pool, major credit cards, nightly/weekly rates, senior citizen discount.

Best Western Bradenton Resort Inn 2303 1st Street W., Bradenton 33508; (813) 747-6465. 241 rooms, pool, restaurant, lounge, laundry. Near shopping and beaches. All major credit cards, senior citizen discount, nightly/weekly rates.

Days Inn 3506 1st Street W., Bradenton 33505; (813) 746-1141. 134 rooms, pool, restaurant, cable, pets, major credit cards, senior citizen discount.

Econo Lodge 6627 U.S. 41, Bradenton 33507; (813) 758-7199. 79 rooms, pool, cable, nightly/weekly rates.

Holiday Inn Riverfront 100 Riverfront Drive W., Bradenton 33505; (813) 747-3727. Riverfront on the edge of downtown next to city park. Jog and walk trails, fishing pier, heated pool, restaurant, all major credit cards.

Ramada Inn Airport 6545 North Tamiami Trail, Sarasota 34243; (813) 355-7771. 110 rooms, restaurant with northern Italian cuisine, lounge with comedy club. Continental breakfast, pool, cable, pets, major credit cards, senior citizen discount.

All of the following feature an island gulf front with private beaches:
Bali Hai Resort   6900 Gulf Drive, Holmes Beach 33510; (813) 778-6604.
42 rooms and apartments, pool, cable, laundry, nightly/weekly rates.
Catalina Beach Resort   1325 Gulf Drive N., Bradenton Beach 33510;
(813) 778-6611. 32 rooms and apartments. Sailboat rentals, pool, night-
ly/weekly rates, major credit cards.
Holiday Inn/Holidome Longboat Key   4949 Gulf of Mexico Drive,
Longboat Key 33548; (813) 383-3771. 146 rooms, indoor pool, two restaurants, two lounges with entertainment, tennis, cable, pets, all credit
cards.
Longboat Key Hilton   4711 Gulf of Mexico Drive, Longboat Key
33548; (813) 383-2451. 102 rooms and efficiencies, pool, restaurant,
lounge, entertainment, tennis, all credit cards.
Resort Sixty-Six   6600 Gulf Drive N., Holmes Beach 33510; (813)
778-2238. 42 rooms, apartments, and efficiencies. Pool, restaurant,
cable, spa.
Sand & Sea   2412 Gulf Drive, Bradenton Beach 33510; (813) 778-2231.
30 rooms, apartments, and efficiencies; pool; nightly/weekly rates.
The Coconuts   100 73rd Street, Holmes Beach 33510; (813) 778-2277.
27 rooms and one- or two-bedroom apartments, pool, cable, two-night
minimum, all major credit cards.

MORSELS   As in most areas in Florida, dining in Manatee County
ranges from avoidable to irresistible. There are the usual assortment
of fast-food joints, as well as some truly fine dining experiences . . .
with a delectable selection of seafood from the county's own fishing
villages.
Call Us Cajun   3812 Manatee Avenue W., Bradenton; (813) 747-4183.
Downtown location, great prices. Award-winning cajun food reflecting
its Louisiana heritage.
Euphemia Haye Restaurant   5540 Gulf of Mexico Drive, Longboat
Key; (813) 383-3633. Intimate atmosphere for excellent French cuisine.
Fast Eddy's Place   101 Bay Boulevard S., Bradenton; (813) 778-2251.
On Anna Maria Island. This is a very popular eatery, with fresh seafood
(try the oysters), low prices, and large quantities.
Seafood Shack   Cortez Road at the Intracoastal Waterway; (813)
794-1235. Casual waterfront dining at nice prices.
L'Auberge du bon Vivant   7003 Gulf of Mexico Drive, Longboat Key;
(813) 383-2421. Fine French cuisine prepared by chef/owner. Reservations recommended.

NO PIE IN THE SKY

My first spring training with the Pirates was in 1922 at Hot Springs, Arkansas. We stayed downtown at the Eastmont Hotel, and each day we took a trolley car to the playing field, where manager George Gibson held two workouts a day from 10:00 A.M. to noon and again from 1:30 to 3:00 P.M. Between sessions, we trekked back to the Eastmont for lunch. There were no clubhouse, locker room, or shower facilities at the training site, so after practice each day we had strict orders to take a bath at the hotel in the basement. We hung our uniform near an open window in our hotel room, hoping it would dry out for the next day's practice.

''We played only thirteen exhibition games, traveling by train to such cities as Shreveport, Louisiana; Little Rock, Arkansas; and Memphis, Tennessee—wherever a major league or minor league club might be training. When traveling, each player was given $3.75 a day for meals. . . . We never even thought about bringing our wives or families south with us, and the silent movies were about the only break in our training routine. I guess you could say that things have changed a lot. . . .''
—**Pie Traynor, Pirate Hall-of-Famer**

Sandbar 100 Spring Avenue, Anna Maria Island; (813) 778-7595. Specialty is fresh native seafood. Very scenic deck on the beach. You could even call it romantic.

Moore's Stone Crab Restaurant & Marina 800 Broadway, Longboat Key; (813) 383-1748. Family owned. Some call its stone crab the best on Florida's west coast. Famous for Jackie the Dolphin, who does tricks for customers on the Intracoastal Waterway.

Candelino's Italian Restaurant Tower Square, 5603 Manatee Avenue W., Bradenton; (813) 792-1886. Southern Italian dinners. Flaming dinners, desserts, and coffee prepared at your table. Reservations recommended.

The Fish Net 4027 Cortez Road W., Bradenton; (813) 755-4214. Specializing in fresh seafood. Carryout service. Call ahead for takeout. Oyster bar.

ATTRACTIONS Despite some overdevelopment, such as on the Tamiami Trail, Manatee County has escaped many of the negative effects of Florida's booming and often out-of-control growth. Beaches are largely clean and white (though Anna Maria can be dirty and crowded), with views unmarred by high-rise condos or hotels. And what views: the Gulf of Mexico's blue-green waters, rolling white dunes dotted with sea oats, and a border of Australian pines.

Shelling is abundant, and many travelers can find perfect sand dollars or scallop-shaped shells from the numerous county public beaches on Anna Maria Island and Longboat Key.

For those who enjoy more active beach pursuits, the area offers a variety of boat docks, marinas, fishing piers, boat tours, and boat charters. Swimming, waterskiing, sailing, canoeing, windsurfing, and scuba diving are other possibilities.

Anna Maria Bayfront Park Located at the northern end of Anna Maria Island, this secluded beach fronts both the Intracoastal Waterway and the Gulf of Mexico. Complete recreational facilities. Take Manatee Avenue (State Road 64) from Bradenton to Anna Maria Island.

Coquina Beach Coquina is a popular beach on the southern end of Anna Maria Island. Take West Cortez (County Road 684) from Bradenton to Gulf Drive (County Road 789) on Anna Maria Island. Take Gulf Drive south to the beach.

Cortez Beach On Gulf Boulevard, Cortez is a three-quarter-mile stretch of beach located on Anna Maria Island.

Lake Manatee State Recreational Area This 556-acre park is spread along three miles of the south shore of Lake Manatee, a man-made reservoir. Facilities include boating, beach, picnic area, and swimming area watched by lifeguards. The park is located about five miles east of I-75 on State Road 64. Information: (813) 746-8042.

Longboat Key   The key is literally a continuous stretch of sand. Several secluded beaches are reachable by driving to the end of narrow, east-west roads leading through ritzy residential neighborhoods (located south of Santa Maria Island on County Road 789). Information: (813) 383-1212.

Inland Manatee County features the city of Bradenton (population 40,000) and its many historical sites, museums, special annual events, fine restaurants, and shopping. The county civic center draws name entertainers and is the hub of social and business events.

DeSoto National Memorial   This memorial park takes visitors back to the sixteenth century and the days of Hernando de Soto's exploration of the southeastern United States. Located five miles west of Bradenton on State Road 64 (on Tampa Bay). Hours are 8:00 A.M. to 5:30 P.M. daily. Admission is by donation.

Operated by the U.S. Department of the Interior, park employees in period dress demonstrate the use of various sixteenth-century weapons and show how food was prepared and preserved for extended explorations. A half-mile nature trail ambles through the park, circling a mangrove jungle. Movies are shown on the hour. Information: (813) 792-0458.

Braden Castle Park   Located on 27th Street and State Road 64 in Bradenton at the confluence of the Braden and Manatee rivers, the park contains the ruins of Braden Castle. Built by sugar planter Joseph Braden, the castle—one of the earliest plantation houses in the county—is the source of the city of Bradenton's name. The castle is recognized on the National Register of Historic Homes.

The park is open from sunrise to sunset, free of charge. Information: (813) 746-7700.

South Florida Museum   The museum includes more than 50,000 square feet of exhibition space depicting Florida history from the age of the dinosaurs to the space age. The museum houses one of the finest collections of Civil War memorabilia in the United States.

Located at 201 10th Street West in Bradenton, the museum is open from 10:00 A.M. to 5:00 P.M. Tuesday through Friday, and 1:00 P.M. to 5:00 P.M. on weekends. Closed Mondays.

Admission (museum only): adults $2; children and students $1.25; preschoolers free. Admission to the museum and the Bishop Planetarium (located in the same building): adults $3; children and students $2. No preschoolers admitted to the planetarium. Information: (813) 746-4131.

The Bishop Planetarium contains a fifty-foot hemispherical dome that arcs above the seating area. In the center stands a star projector that can depict the sky as seen from anywhere in our solar system. Star shows 1:30 and 3:00 P.M. Tuesday through Sunday; 7:30 P.M. Friday and Saturday.

Gamble Plantation State Historical Site   On U.S. Highway 301 in Ellenton, just north of Bradenton; (813) 722-1017.

Madira Bickel Mound   A ten-acre site at the foot of the Sunshine Skyway Bridge between Bradenton and St. Petersburg, containing shell mounds and the remains of several ancient Indian burial grounds; (813) 722-1017.

Manatee Heritage Week   Held annually in the last full week of March at historical sites throughout Manatee County. Area historical groups sponsor guided tours.

When you're not watching the Pirates but feel in a sporting mood, you can golf, play tennis, or even go horseback riding.

Heather Hills Golf Club   101 Cortez Road W., Bradenton (has driving range).

Manatee County Golf Course   5100 64th Street W., Bradenton (has driving range).

Palm View Hills Golf Course   5712 28th Avenue E., Palmetto.

Palma Sola Golf Course   3807 75th Street W., Bradenton.

Palmetto Pines Golf Course   Golf Course Road, Parrish.

Santa Rosa Country Club   6611 Cortez Road W., Bradenton (has driving range).

Airport Driving Range   1175 General Spaatz Boulevard, Bradenton.

Bayshore Tennis Courts   34th Street W. (next to the high school), Bradenton.

J. P. Miller Tennis Courts   43rd Street, Bradenton.

Ron-Con Horse Ranch   Singletary Road, Myakka City; by appointment only. Call (813) 322-1122.

For more information contact:
Bradenton Chamber of Commerce
222 10th Street
Bradenton 33505
(813) 748-3411

Clearwater

PHILADELPHIA PHILLIES

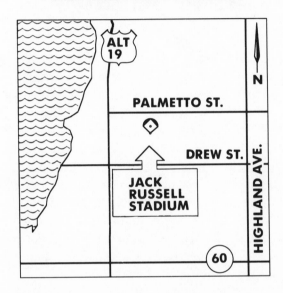

THE TEAM

On February 24, 1947, the Philadelphia Phillies held their first workout in Clearwater. More than four decades later, the team and the town are still going at it.

The Phils open up camp in late February at the Carpenter Complex, about four miles east of Jack Russell Stadium, where the team plays its exhibition schedule.

TEAM HOTEL   Quality Inn, 120 U.S. Highway 19 North, Clearwater 33575; (813) 799-1116.

CARPENTER COMPLEX The complex, a joint venture of the city and the Phillies, consists of four diamonds and support facilities. The Phillies work out there from the opening of camp on or about February 20 through the first week of March. After that, the complex is taken over by the minor league organization: Williamsport, Pennsylvania (AAA), of the International League; Reading, Pennsylvania (AA), of the Eastern League; Clearwater (A) of the Florida State League; Spartanburg, South Carolina (A), of the South Atlantic League; and Utica, New York (A), of the NY–Penn League.

Address and Phone Carpenter Complex, Drew Street and Coachman Road, Clearwater 33515; (813) 799-0503.

JACK RUSSELL STADIUM The major league squad moves to Jack Russell Stadium at the end of the first week in March.

The stadium was dedicated on March 10, 1955, the day the Phillies opened their exhibition season. A crowd of 4209 saw the Phillies beat the Tigers, 4–2, on a two-run double by third baseman Willie Jones.

Baseball Commissioner Ford Frick and league presidents Warren Giles and Will Harridge were on hand for the dedication. Jack Russell, a city commissioner and former major league pitcher who settled in Clearwater following his fifteen-year big-league career, had the job of introducing the baseball notables. In introducing Russell, Mayor Herbert Brown made the surprise announcement that the park was to be named after Russell in recognition of his activities promoting the growth of the city and the building of the stadium.

Still one of the nicer parks in Florida, Jack Russell Stadium has seen many improvements over the years. In 1985, a new home clubhouse was built, and additional seats installed. Current capacity is 5347 — 1912 box, 2435 grandstand, 1000 bleacher.

Box seats cost $5, grandstand $4, bleachers $3 (children $1). Senior citizens get a $1 discount on box and grandstand seats for specific games purchased in advance of game day. Season tickets are available, $65 for box seats and $52 for grandstand. Game time for grapefruit league exhibition games is 1:30 P.M. The ticket office is open from 11:00 A.M. to 3:00 P.M. during all home games and can be reached at (813) 442-8496. Tickets cannot be ordered by phone.

Address and Phone Jack Russell Stadium, 800 Phillies Drive, Clearwater 33515; (813) 441-9941.

GETTING AUTOGRAPHS

In spring training, fans will find players in the most relaxed atmosphere that they'll catch them in all year. Players are easy to find in hotels, poolside at the team hotel, at the park, in restaurants.

In general, players are receptive to signing autographs in the spring. Some little kid with baseball cap askew looks up to the skyscraper heights of a real live, professional ball player and implores with pleading eyes for a signature on a scorecard. Outside of a kitten playing with a ball of yarn, is there anything cuter? But the situation often turns into a catch-22 for the player. If he signs fifty autographs, then the fifty-first will be turned down and walk away disappointed.

Assuming there's not a logjam around the player, the best thing for the fan to do is be polite. Ask nicely. The best approach is to walk up to the player, and say something like this:

"Pardon me, Mr. Schmidt. Do you have time to sign this?" Most of the time, you'll find the player very nice about the whole thing, especially if it's a one-on-one situation.

THE AREA

Located in the Tampa Bay metropolitan area directly on the Gulf of Mexico, Clearwater is a thriving, year-round resort, business, and residential community of 96,000.

With the city's location, visitors can spend as much time as they wish on the miles of largely clean, white beaches, yet still remain close to other attractions. The town is easily accessible by car, with Tampa International Airport and St. Petersburg/Clearwater International Airport providing both domestic and international air transportation. Limousine service and rental cars are available at both airports.

BEDDING DOWN   Clearwater has lodgings of every sort with its variety of motels, hotels, resorts, condos, campgrounds, and mobile home parks. Here are a few:

Adam's Mark Caribbean Gulf Resort   430 South Gulfview Boulevard, Clearwater Beach 33515; (813) 443-5714. 207 units, all major credit cards, restaurant, and lounge.

Best Western Sea Wake Inn   691 South Gulfview Boulevard, Clearwater Beach 33515; (813) 443-7652. 100 rooms, all major credit cards, restaurant, and lounge.

Clearwater Beach Hilton   715 South Gulfview Boulevard, Clearwater Beach 33515; (813) 447-9566. 210 units, all major credit cards, restaurant, lounge, walk to shopping.

Clearwater Downtown Travelodge   711 Cleveland Street, Clearwater 33515; (813) 446-9183. 48 units, all major credit cards, restaurant, downtown location near shopping.

Continental Inn   12810 U.S. 19 South, Clearwater 33546; (813) 536-6578. 66 units, efficiencies, all major credit cards, restaurant, lounge.

Gulf Sands Beach Resort   655 Gulfview Boulevard, Clearwater Beach 33515; (813) 442-7171. 152 rooms, all major credit cards, restaurant, lounge, near shopping.

Holiday Inn Central   400 U.S. 19 North, Clearwater 33575; (813) 797-8173. 194 units, all major credit cards, restaurant, lounge, shopping, central location.

Holiday Inn Gulfview   521 Gulfview Boulevard, Clearwater Beach 33515; (813) 447-6461. 288 units, all major credit cards, restaurant, lounge, walk to beach.

Holiday Inn St. Petersburg/Clearwater   3535 Ulmerton Road, Clearwater 33520; (813) 577-9100. 178 rooms, all major credit cards, restaurant, lounge.

Howard Johnson's Motor Lodge 410 U.S. 19 North, Clearwater 33575; (813) 797-5021. Rooms and efficiencies, all major credit cards, restaurant, lounge, close to shopping.

Lagoon Resort Motel 619 South Gulfview Boulevard, Clearwater Beach 33515; (813) 442-5107. 66 units, efficiencies, all major credit cards, restaurant, walk to beach.

Ramada Inn Central 401 U.S. 19 South, Clearwater 33575; (813) 799-1181. 114 units, all major credit cards, restaurant, lounge, near shopping.

Ramada Inn Countryside 2560 U.S. 19 North, Clearwater 33575; (813) 796-1234. 130 units, all major credit cards, restaurant, lounge, near shopping.

Sheraton Sand Resort 1160 Gulf Boulevard, Clearwater Beach 33515; (813) 595-1161. 390 units, all major credit cards, restaurant, lounge, shopping, walk to beach.

Condos Bayshore Apartments, 669 Bay Esplanade, Clearwater Beach 33515; (813) 441-8834. Six units, one bedroom/one bath or efficiency/one bath; weekly or monthly rates; walk to beach.

MORSELS Typical fast food, fresh seafood, buffets, cafeterias, steaks, elegant restaurants: all provide a complete menu for Clearwater eating. Ethnic food includes Greek, Italian, Chinese, Japanese, German, French, and Mexican.

Kapok Tree Restaurant 923 McMullen Booth Road, Clearwater; (813) 776-0504. Noon to 10:00 P.M. Reservations requested.

Tio Pepe Restaurante 2930 Gulf to Bay Boulevard, Clearwater; (813) 799-3082. Fine Mexican cuisine.

Arigato Japanese Steakhouse 1500 U.S. Highway 19 North, Clearwater; (813) 799-0202. Food prepared tableside.

Capt. Anderson II Clearwater Beach Marina, Clearwater Beach; (813) 462-2628. Dinner cruise—departs 7:00 P.M., returns 10:00 P.M.— Tuesday through Saturday. Reservations required.

Lemon Tree Restaurant 2519 McMullen Booth Road, Clearwater; (813) 725-5724. Varied cuisine.

Four Coins Restaurant 1849 Gulf to Bay Boulevard, Clearwater; (813) 461-7610. Varied cuisine.

Alfano's Authentic Italian Restaurant 1704 Clearwater-Largo Road, Clearwater; (813) 584-2125. Continental cooking.

Bob Heilman's Beachcomber   447 Mandalay Avenue, Clearwater Beach; (813) 442-4144. Continental cuisine on the beach.

China House Restaurants   1411 Gulf to Bay Boulevard, Clearwater; (813) 446-9443. Chinese.

Clearwater Beach Seafood   37 Causeway Boulevard, Clearwater Beach; (813) 443-3057. Seafood specialties and carryout.

Dock of the Bay   735 South Bayway Boulevard, Clearwater Beach; (813) 446-1137. Seafood specialties.

El Madrid Restaurante   415 Cleveland Street, Clearwater; (813) 447-2211. Continental cuisine.

L & N Seafood Grill   2566 Countryside Boulevard, Clearwater; (813) 796-3578. Seafood.

Lenora's   In the Best Western Sea Wake Inn, 691 South Gulfview Boulevard, Clearwater Beach; (813) 443-7652. Seafood.

New Orleans Restaurant and Lounge   1721 Gulf to Bay Boulevard, Clearwater; (813) 443-7608. Varied cuisine.

Peking Palace of Far East   1608 Gulf to Bay Boulevard, Clearwater; (813) 461-4414. Chinese cuisine.

Penrod's of Clearwater   2543 Countryside Boulevard, Clearwater; (813) 796-7115.

Showboat Dinner Theater   3405 Ulmerton Road, Clearwater; (813) 576-3818. Buffet.

ATTRACTIONS   In Clearwater, situated on the Pinellas County Suncoast, diverse activities include everything from an excellent nightlife to sunning on the beach, from movie theaters to comedy, from shopping to sports, from parades to rock 'n' roll. Here's a partial list of attractions:

Clearwater Beach   More than three miles of soft, sparkling white sand on the Gulf of Mexico. The beach, bespeckled with tiny ivory-colored shells, can be blinding in the sun, so sunglasses are a must. Activities include swimming, windsurfing, waterskiing, sailing, and fishing. The beach is connected to Clearwater by Memorial Causeway. Don't pick the sea oats; the endangered plants are protected by state law. Information: (813) 446-2424.

Moccasin Lake Nature Park   2750 Park Trail Lane, Clearwater. A remnant of natural woodlands preserved in the middle of a rapidly developing urban area. Information: (813) 462-6024.

Clearwater Marine Science Center and Sea Aquarium   249 Windward Passage, Clearwater. It is the only facility for the rescue and rehabilitation of marine mammals on Florida's west coast, and one of only eight in the nation. Exhibits. Directions: take Memorial Causeway west to the Island Estates traffic light. Turn right onto Island Way. Turn left at the first light and follow the signs. Information: (813) 447-0980.

Performing Arts Center and Theater (PACT)   1111 McMullen Booth Road, Clearwater. Year-round programs offer a variety of performing arts, including professional groups in classic and modern productions. Information: (813) 725-5573.

Royalty Theater Company   405 Cleveland Street, Clearwater. Information: (813) 443-6647.

Little Theatre of Clearwater   302 Seminole Street, Clearwater. Information: (813) 596-8233.

Boatyard Village   1600 Fairchild Drive, Clearwater. More than thirty-six shops with six restaurants overlooking a man-made lake. Information: (813) 535-4678.

Sunshine Mall   Missouri Avenue at Druid Road, Clearwater. Just a few blocks from the beach are more than one hundred stores, including J. C. Penney and J. Byrons. Information: (813) 447-6073.

Countryside Mall   2601 Highway 19 North, Clearwater. This is one of Florida's biggest malls, with over 160 stores and shops. Information: (813) 796-1238.

A Place for Cooks   1447 South Fort Harrison Avenue, Clearwater. A cook's heaven, this 3000-square-foot store has every kitchen gadget ever invented, plus a few that haven't been. Daily cooking demonstrations. Information: (813) 446-5506.

Airco Flite 18   3650 Roosevelt Boulevard, Clearwater. Eighteen holes, par 72. Information: (813) 576-1453.

Clearwater Country Club   525 North Betty Lane, Clearwater. Semi-private, eighteen holes, par 72. Information: (813) 443-5078.

Glen Oaks Country Club   1345 Court Street, Clearwater. Eighteen holes, par 55. Information: (813) 462-6146.

Clearwater Beach Recreation Center   60 Bay Esplanade, Clearwater; (813) 462-6138. Tennis courts.

Downtown Bayfront Municipal Courts   3 Pierce Street, Clearwater; (813) 462-6557. Tennis courts.

Del Oro Park   401 McMullen Booth Road, Clearwater; (813) 462-6148. Tennis courts.

For more information, contact:
Clearwater Chamber of Commerce
128 North Osceola Avenue
Clearwater 33515
(813) 461-0011

Dunedin

TORONTO BLUE JAYS

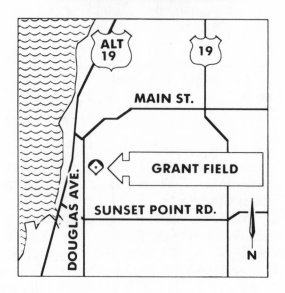

THE TEAM

The Blue Jays have been training in Dunedin for their entire history, going back to 1976. The major league team opens up camp at the Cecil P. Englebert Recreational Complex in the last week of February before switching to Grant Field for the remainder of camp and the exhibition season.

TEAM HOTEL   Ramada Inn, 2560 U.S. 19 North, Clearwater 33575; (813) 796-1234.

THE CECIL P. ENGLEBERT COMPLEX   Jays minor leaguers train here from mid-March to early April. The complex has undergone renovation in the last couple of years, including the addition of three batting tunnels as well as improvements to the fields. A new clubhouse was built, along with a new parking lot and half diamond.

Address and Phone   Englebert Complex, 1700 Solon Avenue, Dunedin 33528; (813) 733-9387.

GRANT FIELD   Toronto played its first spring game here on March 11, 1976, defeating the New York Mets 3-1. Over the years, the Blue Jays have invested about $2.5 million in Grant Field. Prior to 1984, the distances to the outfield were altered. The left field foul pole line was moved closer to the stands, thus adding more distance to right field. Right is now 315 feet from the plate, left 335 feet (this compares to the former dimensions of 301 and 345 feet respectively). Straight-away center is 400 feet, with the left and right field alleys 380 and 365 feet respectively. A net was placed atop the 12-foot fence to save base-balls. Any ball hit into the net is a home run. Other improvements have included the grading and resodding of the field.

For the 1985 season, the Blue Jays switched dugouts and a new home-team clubhouse was built on the third base side. The team's public relations trailer was also replaced by a permanent complex adjacent to the home clubhouse. The facility houses a conference room, PR offices, and a media workroom.

Grant Field is located in a busy area, with a lot of commercial activity around it. Allow yourself plenty of time to get in and out of the park for games, which begin at 1:30 P.M.

The pregame batting schedule at Grant Field works like this: The Blue Jays hit until 11:35 A.M. The visitors hit until 12:35 P.M. Toronto takes its infield practice from 12:35 to 12:50 P.M. The visitors take infield from 12:50 to 1:05 P.M.

Tickets for all Blue Jays games at Dunedin are available through the mail by sending $4 (U.S. funds) per grandstand seat plus a $2 (U.S. funds) per order handling charge to Jays Tickets, City of Dunedin, P.O. Box 1348, Dunedin 34296-1348. Make checks payable to the City of Dunedin. The ticket office at Grant Field is open from late February through the rest of spring training. Hours are 11:00 A.M. to 2:00 P.M. Monday through Saturday. No telephone orders will be accepted. For information, call (813) 733-0429.

When Toronto breaks camp, Grant Field is used by the minor leagues. During the summer, the stadium is home of the Dunedin Blue Jays, Toronto's entry in the Florida State League.

Address and Phone Grant Field, 311 Douglas Avenue, Dunedin 33528; (813) 733-9302.

THE AREA

Dunedin, a small almost villagelike town, is located in the heart of Florida's western Suncoast. Founded in 1870, it is the oldest town on the state's Gulf Coast. The city received its name from two Scottish settlers in 1882, who petitioned their government for a post office to be named "Dunedin," for their native Edinburgh, Scotland. "Dun" means rock and "Edin" means castle, literally, "Castle on the Rock."

The Scottish tradition has been honored in street names, and its influence can be detected in the local architecture.

Many visitors find Dunedin an ideal location. As a small city, it has the appearance and appeal of a sleepy coastal town. Yet, just a short drive away are the major cities of Tampa and St. Petersburg, with all the opportunities for sightseeing, activities, nightlife, culture, and dining.

The city's western coastline stretches for four miles along St. Joseph's Sound. A string of barrier islands separates the sound from the Gulf of Mexico, with several passes linking the two bodies. Dunedin, with a population of 35,000, is located in Pinellas County, a county that forms a peninsula bounded on the east by Tampa Bay and on the west by the Gulf of Mexico. It is Florida's second smallest county in terms of land area (280 square miles), but it's also the most densely populated (4.4 persons per acre).

Driving Mileages from Dunedin to Other Florida Cities Cypress Gardens . . . 76. Daytona Beach . . . 176. Ft. Lauderdale . . . 273. Ft. Meyers . . . 136. Gainesville . . . 127. Haines City . . . 76. Homosassa Springs . . . 60. Jacksonville . . . 195. Key West . . . 394. Melbourne . . . 106. Marineland . . . 212. Miami . . . 264. Ocala . . . 98. Orlando . . . 112. Plant City . . . 42. St. Augustine . . . 185. St. Petersburg . . . 21. Sarasota . . . 65. Silver Springs . . . 104. Tampa . . . 22. Weeki Wachee . . . 38. Winter Haven . . . 73.

Climate Situated as it is, directly on the Gulf of Mexico, Dunedin's weather is tempered in winter and cooled in summer by the close proximity of the Gulf's water and its breezes. About fifty inches of rain falls each year. The average yearly temperature is 71.2 degrees.

FLORIDA VS. ARIZONA

Williams vs. DiMaggio . . . Mantle vs. Mays . . . artificial turf vs. grass . . . Florida vs. Arizona. Debates in baseball can rage for years with nothing ever really being solved. But there is a consensus among most (not all, but most) baseball people that Florida has a decided advantage over Arizona as a place to train.

"There are three reasons why Arizona is not a good place to train, at least, compared to Florida. First, the Arizona air is so thin the balls react like golf balls. They just jump out of the parks. I remember the Mariners played Milwaukee over at Campadre Stadium in Chandler, and the two teams hit fourteen home runs in one game. It's hard to believe that the ball carries like that, but it does. The second major difference between Arizona and Florida is the skies. In Arizona, the skies are so high. You look up, and it looks like it goes on forever. I've seen many good defensive outfielders like Brett Butler and Rick Manning lose balls in the sky. The third factor is perspiration. You can't hold a sweat in Arizona. You dry out too quick because of the air."
—Lou Gorman, general manager, Boston Red Sox

"The players didn't like Arizona because they couldn't sweat. I remember Bill Monbouquette. He was one of the hardest working guys I ever saw anywhere. And he'd work out, work out, and he'd sweat for two minutes, and then he'd dry right out. You couldn't lose weight, and you couldn't get loose out there. The pitchers hated it."
—Tim Horgan, columnist *The Boston Herald*

BEDDING DOWN   Many visitors to the Dunedin area actually stay in nearby towns, such as Clearwater, Clearwater Beach, St. Petersburg, and even Tampa. But you can stay right in Dunedin if you want to. **Amberle Motel**   1035 Broadway Street, Dunedin; (813) 733-3228. 22 units plus one- and two-bedroom efficiencies, pool, all major credit cards.
Sailwinds   1414 Bayshore Boulevard (Alt. 19), Dunedin; (813) 734-8854. Fully furnished studio and one-bedroom units, with gallery-style kitchenettes. Nightly, weekly, or monthly rates.
Braemer Motel   1550 Main Street, Dunedin; (813) 734-2732. Senior citizen discount.
Causeway Motel   2624 North Paula Drive, Dunedin; (813) 734-1374 or 733-3135. Located on Dunedin Causeway, this place has a private fishing-and-boat dock. Three minutes to golf, shopping.
Holiday House Motel   1220 Main Street, Dunedin; (813) 733-5496. Rooms and efficiencies. Near shopping, restaurants.
Jamaica Inn Motel   150 Marina Plaza, Dunedin; (813) 733-4121. On the gulf. Deluxe rooms and suites, pool, restaurant, lounge, weekly and monthly rates. All major credit cards.
Wal-Mar Apartment Motel   1405 Bayshore Boulevard, Dunedin; (813) 733-1783. 8 one-bedroom apartments, by the week or month.
Tides Hotel and Bath Club Resort   16700 Gulf Boulevard, North Reddington Beach; (813) 391-9681. Private beach, golf course.

MORSELS
Bill's Lighthouse   813 Dodecanese Boulevard (Sponge Docks), Tarpon Springs; (813) 938-4895. Greek dining and seafood (everything from oysters to octopus). Moderate to inexpensive ($4.25 to $11.95). Large bar and lounge.
Bon Appetit   148 Marina Plaza, Dunedin; (813) 733-2151. Award-winning dining. Steak, veal, seafood, and ethnic food. Moderate to expensive ($6.25 to $16.95). Table d'hôte (complete dinners) are popular and less expensive than the regular menu.
Marco Polo   2298 Main Street (State Road 580), Dunedin; (813) 733-3800. Oriental cuisine, with a twenty-five-entrée menu that includes beef sate marinated in wine, garlic, and sesame oil and brushed with peanut sauce. Moderate to expensive ($4.95 to $24.95).
Pappa's Restaurant   10 West Dodecanese Boulevard, Tarpon Springs; (813) 937-5101. Menu emphasizes fresh seafood. The Greek salad and dishes are a specialty also. Moderate to expensive ($3.95 to $16.95).

Sabals 315 Main Street, Dunedin; (813) 734-3463. Forty seats for intimate dining. Reservations a must. Imaginative eating — octopus with feta cheese and olive oil, garlic soup, and chicken stuffed with herbed butter are just a few of the dishes. Moderate to expensive ($12.50 to $18).

Sally's 2901 U.S. Alternate Highway 19 (intersection of Alternate 19 and Alderman Road), Palm Harbor; (813) 784-8788. A varied menu, from New York steaks to fried catfish. The lounge features dancing. Moderate ($5.95 to $11.95).

Steak and Ale 2301 U.S. Highway 19 North, Palm Harbor; (813) 786-2286. Steaks, large salad bar. Dinner comes with soup and bread. Dessert specialty is mudd pie. Moderate to expensive ($5.95 to $16.95).

Trapper's Café and Oyster Bar 537 Douglas Avenue, Dunedin; (813) 736-2986. A family operation with a regular following. Seafood . . . plus more seafood (Ipswich clams, Danish lobster tails). Inexpensive to moderate ($2.95 to $11.95).

ATTRACTIONS Activities in Dunedin definitely take on an outdoor flavor, with boating, swimming, fishing, golf, tennis offered. Dunedin ranks as one of the top fishing spots in Florida, offering both inshore fishing in the bays and inlets, as well as offshore in the Gulf of Mexico. Dunedin is known for its catches of snook, trout, redfish, and tarpon. The reefs — just a short run into the gulf — produce grouper, snapper, trout, kingfish, and mackerel. Access to all of the area's fishing is available to visitors — from the largest sports fishing charter boats venturing far offshore to the smallest rental skiffs for bay fishing.

Highlander Pool The pool, located at Fisher Field, is one of the finest swimming and diving complexes to be found anywhere in the state. It is "L" shaped with a separate training pool and is situated on three acres in a beautiful park setting. There are bathhouses, and the complex is open to the public year round. During the winter and spring months, the pool is heated. A 1.35-mile jogging track and Parcour Course with eighteen exercise stations surround the pool area.

Dunedin Community Center, Stirling Recreation Center, and Highlander Park All three are home to numerous ongoing cultural and recreational activities as well as special events, such as the annual home show in March at Stirling Center and the Dunedin Highland Games in March/April. Call the chamber of commerce for more information.

The Dunedin Fine Arts and Cultural Center A public, nonprofit group that offers cultural activities and programs to the public. Included are free public exhibitions that change monthly and a variety of classes for all age groups. The center also serves as an information hub for the arts in the Dunedin area. Call the chamber of commerce for more information.

Dunedin Historical Society Museum   341 Main Street, Dunedin. A great railroad museum. Even its location is right, in the city's old rail station. Open Tuesday and Saturday 11:00 A.M. to noon; Thursday 9:30 to 11:30 A.M. Information: (813) 733-1291.

Pinellas County Historical Museum   11909 125th Street N., Largo. Guides in period costumes lead you through an array of historic homes and buildings. You'll see how people lived in the early days of Florida. Open Tuesday through Saturday 10:00 A.M. to 4:00 P.M.; Sunday from 1:00 to 4:00 P.M. Information: (813) 462-3474.

Bingo   Don't laugh. This is the fastest growing wagering game on the Suncoast (faster than the horses, the dogs, and jai alai). How do you find the action? Ask, look for bingo signs, read the newspaper ads. Games are played everywhere, it seems, including churches, fraternal club buildings, mobile home parks, and civic association halls. Prizes run from $50 to $200 a game. You pay $2 to $2.50 for six cards. Many places lay free coffee and donuts on you. For the bingo big time, check out the Seminole Bingo Hall on Orient Road between Hillsborough Avenue and Interstate 4, just east of Tampa before the Florida State Fair grounds. Super jackpots can reach $25,000.

Several par-3 golf layouts are available in the greater Dunedin area (some lighted for night play), and a number of new "executive" courses have been developed. These are longer and more challenging than the par 3s, but not as demanding as the full-length championship courses. Call the chamber of commerce for more information on golf courses, as well as for the location of tennis courts.

Dunedin Country Club   1050 Palm Boulevard, Dunedin. Semiprivate, eighteen holes, par 72. This was formerly a national PGA golf course. An excellent course, well run with full facilities.

Sun Ni Land Golf   State Road 580, Dunedin. Public, nine holes, men par 54, women par 64.

For more information, contact:
Greater Dunedin Chamber of Commerce
434 Main Street
Dunedin 33528
(813) 736-1550

Port Charlotte

TEXAS RANGERS

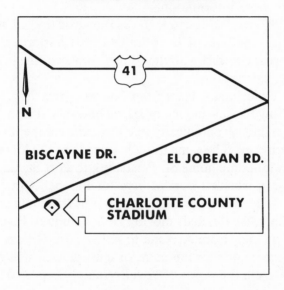

THE TEAM

The Rangers moved their training site from Pompano Beach to Port Charlotte beginning in the spring of 1987. The $5.6 million baseball complex, built for the team by Charlotte County, covers eighty-two acres and houses both the major league and minor league camps. Charlotte County Stadium also serves as home of the Charlotte Rangers in the Florida State League, as well as the site of autumn Instructional League activity.

TEAM HOTEL Island Harbor Resort, 7092 Placida Road, Cape Haze 33946; (813) 697-4800.

CHARLOTTE COUNTY STADIUM The county stadium is at the heart of the Ranger facility. Groundbreaking for the stadium was on April 9, 1986, and construction continued right up until the camp was officially opened in February 1987. The park seats 5000.

Lying beyond the right field fence of the stadium are 5½ practice fields. A control tower, where Ranger brass can make their evaluations, sits at the hub of the four main practice diamonds.

Everything at the site is state of the art—the clubhouses, press facilities, offices, and batting cages.

Ticket prices range from $4 to $6. Call the ticket office at (813) 625-9500 for more information.

Prior to 1987, the Washington/Texas franchise trained in Pompano Beach, Florida. As part of its move to Port Charlotte, the Rangers signed a ten-year contract with the county for use of the facility. There are two five-year options.

The county's luring the team from Pompano Beach is indicative of a trend affecting Florida and major league baseball. Since a team means so much to an area economically (see box), the competition for franchises is heating up. The same thing happened to the Mets, who were coaxed from longtime home St. Petersburg to Port St. Lucie in 1988, and the Royals, who left Fort Meyers for Baseball City.

Rumors of team moves are almost as hot as trade talk come March in Florida. Talk has the Reds moving from Tampa to Plant City, and the Indians moving from Arizona to either Fort Meyers, Tampa, or Pompano Beach. Look for this game of musical franchises to continue.

To borrow from the words of Yogi Berra as he reported to his umpteenth spring camp: "It's déjà vu, all over again."

Address and Phone Charlotte County Stadium, 2300 El Jobean Road, Port Charlotte 33948; (813) 625-9500.

THE AREA

Port Charlotte in Charlotte County is located on the southern Gulf Coast of Florida, about one hundred miles south of Tampa on U.S. Highway 41 (also known as the Tamiami Trail). About twenty-four miles to the south is Fort Meyers. Miami is 160 miles southeast. A fine road system makes the county a traversible one: U.S. Highway 17 ends in the county, with I-75 open from the Route 301 interchange north of Riverview to Alligator Alley. There are five county interchanges along I-75, two north of the Peace River, and three south of it.

With a subtropical climate, an annual average temperature of 74.8 degrees, and the beachline, the area is a popular one for travelers.

Port Charlotte is in the midst of a population explosion, a fact attendant upon rapid development. Today, there are between 55,000 and 60,000 residents. About twenty-five years ago, the land they live on was all cattle pasture.

A yacht club, several shopping areas, two eighteen-hole country clubs, and a cultural center provide plenty of diversity.

BEDDING DOWN
Charlotte Bay Resort & Club 23128 Bayshore Road, Charlotte Harbor; (813) 627-2300. Two-bedroom, two-bath condo units, fully furnished. Rentals by day (minimum two days), week, month, or season.
Port Charlotte Motel 3491 Tamiami Trail, Port Charlotte; (813) 625-4177. Located in the heart of the city, with deluxe rooms and efficiencies, pool, and docks for fishing and boating.
Doc Potts Waterfront Motel 23141 Bayshore Road, Charlotte Harbor; (813) 627-6262.
Econo Lodge 1520 Tamiami Trail, Punta Gorda; (813) 639-8000.
Harbour Inn 5000 Tamiami Trail, Charlotte Harbor; (813) 625-6126.
Holiday Inn 300 West Retta Esplanade, Punta Gorda; (813) 639-1165.
Howard Johnson's Motor Lodge 33 Tamiami Trail, Punta Gorda; (813) 639-2167.
Ramada Inn 3400 Tamiami Trail, Port Charlotte; (813) 625-4181.
Richard's Apartment Village 4335 Sibley Bay Street, Charlotte Harbor; (813) 625-4485.
Sand Piper Motel 3291-A Tamiami Trail, Port Charlotte; (813) 625-4016.
Sea Cove 900 East Marion Avenue, Punta Gorda; (813) 639-0600.
Sun Lake Villa 4800 Tamiami Trail, Charlotte Harbor; (813) 625-1339.

MORSELS
Gerace's Restaurant 2315 Tamiami Trail, Port Charlotte; (813) 629-7779.
Giorgio's Restaurant 2665 Tamiami Trail, Port Charlotte; (813) 627-5156.
Golden City Restaurant & Lounge 4536 Tamiami Trail, Charlotte Harbor; (813) 629-3311.
Joshua's 1105 Taylor Road, Punta Gorda; (813) 639-5333.

THE NAME OF THE GAME IS MONEY

Charlotte County lured the Rangers to Pompano Beach by building a $5.6 million training complex for the team. Why such *largesse*? In a word, money.

It is estimated that major league baseball impacts on Florida to the tune of about $100 million. That's a conservative estimate. In 1986, the Florida Office of Tourism estimated that between $500 million and $1 billion (billion with a ''b'') are injected into the state by baseball!

A team can be expected to spend directly about a half million in its host town. But that's just the beginning. The tourists who come to town for baseball will drop another $7 million to $8 million in hotels, motels, restaurants, attractions, and retail shops.

These are big-league numbers, and as communities realize the economic importance of baseball, competition for franchises will increase. Sweetheart deals will be offered, and cities that now have major league teams will have to play ball to keep them.

Marty's Village Restaurant   3245 Tamiami Trail, Port Charlotte; (813) 625-0990.

Mexican Hacienda   123 East Retta Esplanade, Punta Gorda; (813) 639-7161.

Mister B's   3222 Tamiami Trail, Port Charlotte; (813) 629-7555.

Ping's Chinese Cuisine   4109 Tamiami Trail, Port Charlotte; (813) 627-2233.

Potts' Hot Dogs   2320 Tamiami Trail, Port Charlotte; (813) 624-3700.

Promenade Rib & Steak House   3280-10 Tamiami Trail, Port Charlotte; (813) 625-8880.

Rheinlander Haus   3626 Tamiami Trail, Port Charlotte; (813) 629-8884.

Ria's Ristorante   21202 Olean Road, Port Charlotte; (813) 625-3145.

Riverhouse Restaurant   5114 Melbourne Street, Charlotte Harbor; (813) 629-0007.

Riviera Oyster Bar   5500 Deltona Drive, Punta Gorda; (813) 639-2633.

Smitty's Beef Room   3883 Tamiami Trail, Port Charlotte; (813) 625-4900.

Village Oyster Bar   1200 West Retta Esplanade, Punta Gorda; (813) 637-1212.

ATTRACTIONS   Port Charlotte offers the advantages of a variety of activities, great fishing, and a relatively quiet Florida experience.

Port Charlotte Cultural Center   2280 Aaron Street, Port Charlotte; (813) 625-6155. The focal point for the county's educational, cultural, recreational, and social activities. The complex includes a 418-seat theater with a full slate of concerts, plays, films, and lectures.

Fisherman's Village Marina   1200 West Retta Esplanade, Punta Gorda; (813) 639-8721. Located at the Punta Gorda city dock, the village includes seven restaurants, a swimming pool, rental condos, boat rentals, and more than forty shops.

Charlotte County Memorial Auditorium   75 Taylor Street, Punta Gorda; (813) 639-5833. This showplace overlooking the Peace River seats 2000 and hosts all kinds of bills: conventions, arts and crafts shows, stage productions, wrestling, and bands. Close by are motels and a shopping plaza.

Youth Museum of Charlotte County   260 Retta Esplanade, Punta Gorda; (813) 639-3777. A hands-on museum with changing displays and exhibits, from doll displays to real lions, birds, and snakes. Films, field trips, and instruction mean a good time for kids. Hours are from 10:00 A.M. to 3:00 P.M. Tuesday through Saturday.

Beaches There are two fine beaches in the area. The first is Englewood Beach, which offers paved parking, rest rooms, concession stand, swimming, and picnicking. At Port Charlotte Beach, there are fishing, docking facilities, a swimming pool, bait and tackle shop, and a playground.

Fishing Numerous places. Your best bet is to call the chamber of commerce. But also try Charlotte Harbor Pier (off Bayshore), Harbor Heights Park (three docks), Charlotte Harbor Fishing Reef (off Hog Island).

Jogging/Fitness Trail Port Charlotte at Kiwanis Park, Midway Boulevard. This is a twenty-station fitness trail. The park has playground, rest room, picnicking, and nature trails.

Picnicking In the Port Charlotte area, picnic grounds are located at Lake Betty Rotary Park on Conway Boulevard; McGuire Park on Elkcam Boulevard; Charlotte Harbor Park on Edgewater Drive; Higgs Park on Higgs Drive; and Kiwanis Park. All areas are equipped with tables and grilles.

Tennis At McGuire Park, four lighted courts; Harbour Heights Park, three lighted courts.

The area's public golf course is Sunnybreeze Palms Golf Course, Route 3, Arcadia; (813) 625-0424. Semiprivate courses include:

Maple Leaf Country Club Kings Highway, Port Charlotte; (813) 629-1666.

Marina Golf Club Burnt Shore Marina, One Matecumbe Key Road, Punta Gorda; (813) 637-1577.

Port Charlotte Country Club 22400 Glen Eagles Terrace, Port Charlotte; (813) 625-4109.

Punta Gorda Country Club Highway 17, Punta Gorda; (813) 639-1494.

PROXIMITY TO MAJOR FLORIDA ATTRACTIONS Other major attractions in Florida are relatively close by. This chart shows where and how far.

Attraction	Route	Driving Time	Miles
Walt Disney World	17N; 60E; 27N; 4E	2½ hours	130
Busch Gardens	I-75N; 672E; 301N	1½ hours	115
Cypress Gardens	17N to Winter Haven	1¼ hours	75

Attraction	Route	Driving Time	Miles
Sea World	17N; 60E; 27N; 4E	2½ hours	135
Thos. Edison Home	41S; 867SW	1 hour	35
African Safari Park	I-75S; 846W; 41S	1½ hours	60
Everglades Gardens	I-75S; 865W; 41N	1¼ hours	50
Ringling Museum	41N	1½ hours	55
Baseball & Boardwalk	17N; 60E; 27N	2 hours	110
Police Museum	41N	10 minutes	10

For more information, contact:
Charlotte County Chamber of Commerce
2702 Tamiami Trail
Port Charlotte 33952
(813) 627-2222

St. Petersburg

ST. LOUIS CARDINALS

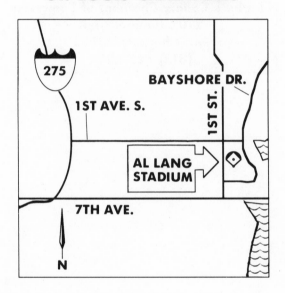

THE TEAM

When two saints get together, the result can be heavenly. Even merely celestial isn't bad. Somewhere in between is what results when these saints—St. Petersburg and St. Louis—come marching into spring baseball.

Camp begins during the last week of February at the Busch Complex, before the big-league team switches to its home park, Al Lang Stadium.

TEAM HOTEL   St. Petersburg Hilton & Towers, 333 First Street S., St. Petersburg 33701; (813) 894-5000.

BUSCH COMPLEX The forty-man roster reports here and, for the first week and a half of camp, holds workouts at Busch. Workouts begin daily at 9:00 A.M. and are free to the public. Keep in mind that, before the exhibition season gets under way, teams begin workouts early in the morning, between 9:00 and 10:00 for most. So don't show up when you would for a game. By 1:30 or 2:00 all the action is over, except for a few workaholics who are doing boring things such as taking batting practice against a pitching machine or running wind sprints. And these hardy stragglers often are lesser lights. At this hour the stars have usually showered and are heading to the golf course.

The Busch Complex has everything needed to conduct a meaningful camp for hundreds of players: multiple diamonds, batting cages, viewing areas, fungo circles, and mounds of fire ants (be careful if you sit on the grass).

Address and Phone Busch Complex, 955 62nd Avenue N.E., St. Petersburg 33702; (813) 522-2108.

AL LANG STADIUM The stadium is located downtown amidst a gaggle of confusing one-way streets. So when heading there for a game (game time is at 1:00 P.M.), give yourself a break and leave early. So you get to the park a little early. You can always use the time to work on your tan.

The stadium, built in 1977 to replace the more sleepy and quaint Al Lang Field, is all concrete, with stands sloping up in a steep, precarious angle. Also beware of the metal seats, which, under a hot Florida sun, can sizzle up and create a stifling, saunalike effect.

Now that Al Lang Stadium sounds like a torture chamber, let's be quick to point out the benefits of watching games here: you can watch the game and at the same time catch glimpses of boats in the bay beyond the fence. The sloped stands afford excellent viewing no matter where you sit. Finally, there is a sense of tradition, of history, in St. Pete. The Yankees used to train here, with men like Ruth, Gehrig, and DiMaggio. So did the old Gas House Cardinals. The pre–World War I Phillies trained here as well, at a field with the delightful name of Coffee Pot Park. The park was named for the free coffee served up to fans.

Tickets at Al Lang Stadium cost $6 for boxes, $4.50 for the grandstand, and $2.50 for bleachers. The ticket office is open daily from 10:00 A.M. beginning on February 28. You can reach the ticket office at (813) 896-4641.

During the summer, Al Lang Field is home to the St. Petersburg Cardinals of the Florida State League (A).

Address and Phone Al Lang Stadium, 180 Second Avenue S.E., St. Petersburg 33701; (813) 894-4773.

THE AREA

Many fans and visitors who come to Florida for spring training like staying in St. Petersburg because it affords them the opportunity of being close to the largest number of camps. Many media people, for example, will use the St. Pete area as a "headquarters" from which they can cover a lot of camps with a minimum amount of travel. Many fans do the same.

St. Petersburg is the cosmopolitan star in a galaxy of resort communities including Tarpon Springs, Dunedin, Clearwater Beach, and Treasure Island. The bustling city wasn't always that way, though. Back in the fifties, when the Yankees trained here, Don Larsen ran his car into a lamppost well after curfew. The following morning, Manager Casey Stengel told the press that Larsen would not be fined for his night out, explaining: "Anyone who can find something to do in St. Petersburg at 5:00 in the morning deserves a medal, not a fine."

Compared with Tampa, the pace of St. Pete is a little slow, but that image is changing as the Suncoast of Florida continues its development boom.

BEDDING DOWN The word variety comes up here. Lodgings range from plain and simple to posh and elegant, from beach hideaways to towering resorts. A list of selected accommodations follows. For a more comprehensive listing, send for the *Suncoast Accommodations Directory*. Mail $1 to the Pinellas Suncoast Tourist Development Council, Newport Square, 2333 East Bay Drive, Suite 109A, Clearwater 33546 or call (813) 530-6452.

The Princess Martha Hotel Fourth Street at First Avenue N., St. Petersburg; (813) 898-9751. The atmosphere of the twenties. Within walking distance of entertainment, shopping, and the waterfront. Elegant. Restaurant, lounge, pool. All major credit cards accepted.

The Colonials 1101 Fourth Street S., St. Petersburg; (813) 896-5016. Motel and apartments. Walking distance to Al Lang Field. Senior citizen discount.

SPRING TIME FOR THE MEN IN BLUE

What's spring training like for an umpire? A time to work on things, just as it is for the players.

"Umps go through the same things as ball players. The main thing is to get your timing down by working games. You learn what we call 'seeing the ball' again. It takes maybe two or three games to get adjusted, to get the strike zone back. You can lose the strike zone in the off-season, just as a hitter can lose his batting eye. It works the same way. That's the reason why umpires need spring training—to sharpen you and get you ready for the regular season."
—**Hank Soar, former longtime ump.**

"The first thing you've got to do is get your body in shape. I think umpires stay in a little bit better shape than ball players, though you sometimes can't tell by looking at us. I try to walk up to six miles a day. You have to get your body in shape, because if you get tired, you lose concentration, and that's when you get in trouble. Then, on the field, you've just got to go back to basics and get your timing down. You also have to study up on the rule book, because you can get flat-out confused on the field, where you don't have time (to consult the book). We've got to make calls just like that. I have never seen two ball games that were alike. You never get to where you've seen it all, because there's always something new that comes up. Thank God we're able to get four heads together to try to weed it all out."
—**Durwood Merrill, American League umpire**

Ponce de León Hotel Central Avenue and Beach Drive, St. Petersburg; (813) 822-4139. 100 rooms, one block to Al Lang Field. Spa beach and pier, café, lounge.

Villa Rica Apartments 324 30th Avenue N., St. Petersburg; (813) 895-2001. Furnished three-bedroom and one-room efficiency apartments; weekly and monthly rates.

Rodeway Inn 401 34th Street N., St. Petersburg; (813) 327-5647. 110 rooms, pool, restaurant, lounge.

Beach Park Motor Inn 300 Beach Drive, St. Petersburg; (813) 898-6325. Overlooking Tampa Bay, walk to Al Lang Field and the Bayfront Center. Deluxe rooms and efficiencies.

Wilson Motel and Apartments 309 Fourth Street S., St. Petersburg; (813) 898-6621. Rooms and efficiency apartments. Fully equipped kitchens. Walk to Al Lang Stadium.

The Hotel McCarthy 326 First Avenue N., St. Petersburg; (813) 822-4141. Rooms with refrigerators and microwaves. Recently renovated. Eight-story building with beautiful views of Tampa Bay.

Banyan Tree Motel 610 Fourth Street N., St. Petersburg; (813) 821-5421. Efficiency apartments in a downtown setting.

Ambassador/Park Plaza/Park Lane Apartments 446 Second Street N., St. Petersburg; (813) 821-6854. Downtown, fully furnished apartments. Close to everything. Glass-enclosed pool with two built-in spas.

Sheraton–St. Pete Marina & Tennis Club 6800 34 Street S., St. Petersburg; (813) 867-1151. Restaurant, lounge, all major credit cards.

TradeWinds 5500 Gulf Boulevard, St. Petersburg Beach; toll free 1-800-237-0707. Resort living on the Gulf of Mexico. Twelve acres of lush courtyards and waterways, deluxe rooms and suites.

Dolphin Beach Resort 4900 Gulf Boulevard, St. Petersburg Beach; toll free 1-800-237-8916. 174 rooms, directly on the beach. Restaurant, lounge.

Holiday Inn 5300 Gulf Boulevard, St. Petersburg Beach; (813) 360-6911. 120 rooms, poolside efficiencies, rooftop dining and dancing, entertainment nightly.

Howard Johnson's 6100 Gulf Boulevard, St. Petersburg Beach; toll free 1-800-237-8918. Directly on the gulf, kitchen units, restaurant.

Holiday Shores 3860 Gulf Boulevard, St. Petersburg Beach; (813) 367-1967. Rooms, apartments, efficiencies.

MORSELS

Aldo's Italian Ristorante 6812 66th Street N., St. Petersburg; (813) 541-2679. Very Italian, with plenty of tableside cooking. The maitre d' flames desserts.

Bahama Bill's 320 Fourth Street N. (in Pennsylvania Hotel), St. Petersburg; (813) 821-4931. An unlikely name for an Italian restaurant, but that's what it is. Chicken cacciatore and veal scalloppini featured. Free fresh fruit bowl served after dinner.

La Côte Basque Winehouse 3104 Beach Boulevard S., Gulfport; (813) 321-6888. Small but nice. Delicious French onion soup. Entrées include shrimp in sherry and baked flounder.

Fat Jacque's Cajun Café 11300 Fourth Street N., St. Petersburg; (813) 578-0158. Cajun and New Orleans cuisine featured. Nice atmosphere.

Ted Peter's Smoked Fish Restaurant 1350 Pasadena Avenue S., South Pasadena; (813) 381-7931. Popular spot for casual dining serving two fish that come right from the Gulf of Mexico: mullet and mackerel.

Charterhouse 1110 Pinellas Bayway, Tierra Verde; (813) 866-2984. Located in Tierra Verde Shopping Center. Featured items are lamb, ribs, lobster tail, and Cornish hens.

Harvey's Fourth Street Grill 3121 Fourth Street N., St. Petersburg; (813) 821-6516. Favorite hangout for the younger set of St. Pete. Pasta, shrimp, scampi, grouper.

Silas Dent's Restaurant and Oyster Bar 5501 Gulf Boulevard, St. Petersburg Beach; (813) 360-6961. Entrées include seafood, and also Florida specialties such as fried alligator strips.

C. Chan's Hilton Inn, 5250 Gulf Boulevard, St. Petersburg Beach; (813) 360-1811. Great view of the gulf, especially at sunset. Seafood dishes, lamb, beef.

Crab Market 9555 Blind Pass Road, St. Petersburg Beach; (813) 360-4656. House specialty is fresh crab.

Peter's Place 208 Beach Drive N.E., St. Petersburg; (813) 822-8436. Dignified, downtown dining. Varied menu that changes daily.

The St. Petersburg area also has four professional dinner theaters. They are the Golden Apple Dinner Theater downtown, the Country Dinner Playhouse in St. Pete's Gateway Mall, the Pinellas Park Showboat Dinner Theater, and the Royal Palm Dinner Theater in Reddington Beach's Bath Club. Call the chamber of commerce for details.

ATTRACTIONS As we said before, St. Pete is chucking its somnambulent image. One bold example is the Suncoast Playboy Club downtown in the back of the Bayfront Concourse Hotel. More in the line of family interests downtown is the bayfront itself. Restaurants, shops of all kinds, observation decks, and its famous pyramid pier jutting into Tampa Bay make it a wonderful place to spend some time when not at the beach or the ballpark. But there are other destinations, too.

The Dali Museum   1000 Third Street S., St. Petersburg; (813) 823-3767. This museum houses the world's largest collection of works by the famous Spanish artist Salvador Dali. Guided tours are held daily, Tuesday through Saturday 10:00 A.M. to 5:00 P.M., and noon to 5:00 P.M. on Sunday. Some 93 oils, 200 watercolors and drawings, and 1000 prints are exhibited.

H.M.S. Bounty   345 Second Avenue N.E., St. Petersburg. This 118-foot-long ship is an exact replica of the ill-fated British ship and was used in the filming of the MGM film *Mutiny on the Bounty* starring Marlon Brando. It has appeared in several other films as well. Guided tours. For more information, call the St. Pete Chamber of Commerce.

Sunken Gardens   1825 Fourth Street N., St. Petersburg; (813) 896-3186. A lush tropical paradise in the heart of downtown. More than 5000 varieties of plants and hundreds of birds, with the largest walk-through aviary in the South. Open daily from 9:00 A.M. to 5:30 P.M..

The Museum of Fine Arts   255 Beach Drive N.E., St. Petersburg; (813) 896-2667. Fine collection of French impressionist artists as well as black and white photographs. Open Tuesday through Saturday, 10:00 A.M. to 5:00 P.M.

Tyrone Square Mall   6901 22nd Avenue N., St. Petersburg; (813) 345-0126. More than 140 stores anchored by Maas Brothers, Robinson's, J. C. Penney, and Sears. Open seven days a week.

Swimsuit Outlet   7116 Gulf Boulevard, St. Petersburg; (813) 367-1545. Top quality swimsuits and outdoor wear. Discounts from 20 to 60 percent. Open daily except for Sunday.

When you've OD'd on baseball, there are lots of other sports to be amused by. In addition to those listed here, you'll find horse racing, auto racing, and ice and roller skating at several indoor rinks.

Golf   St. Pete boasts a multitude of courses, from comfortable par-3 fairways to a plush championship fifty-four-hole green. Mangrove Bay is ranked as one of the top fifty municipal courses nationwide. The pros draw fans to annual spring tournaments such as the S & H Golf Classic at Pasadena Golf and Country Club, the oldest tour in the LPGA circuit. For the locations of the forty courses in Pinellas County, contact the St. Pete Chamber of Commerce.

Dog Racing   This is the Suncoast's most popular spectator sport. St. Petersburg is the location of Derby Lane, the world's oldest, continuously operating greyhound track. Founded in 1925, the track is recognized as one of the finest in the world. More than 1 million fans go to the dogs during Derby Lane's January to May season.

Tennis There are more than 200 courts to choose from in the St. Pete/ Suncoast area. Call the chamber of commerce for a listing.

Fishing The Gulf and Bay waters yield up amberjack, red and gray snapper, flounder, grouper, sea bass, cobia, trigger, sailfish, sea trout, tarpon, mackerel, kingfish, snook. Pier anglers find plenty of room and usually lots of luck at Big Indian Rocks Pier, Fort DeSoto Park Pier, and Pier 60 in Clearwater. For deep-sea fishermen, there are plenty of charter and party boats operating out of St. John's Pass on Madeira Beach and Pass-A-Grille on St. Petersburg Beach. Wading fishermen will love the hundreds of shoal waters and fresh water lakes.

Boating St. Petersburg's peninsula-shaped berth between the waters of the Gulf of Mexico and the Tampa Bay provides some of the best boating to be found anywhere in the country. America's Intercoastal Waterway guides ships from Maine to Florida on the East Coast. When vessels arrive in Florida, the 153-mile Intracoastal Waterway provides protected cruising. The St. Petersburg Municipal Marina is the largest in the state.

Other entertainments include:

Bayfront Center 400 First Street S., St. Petersburg; (813) 893-7211. This showplace holds 2300 in its theater and 8500 in the arena. Events include Broadway musicals, concerts, opera, the circus, ballet, drama, ice shows, wrestling, and more . . . everyone from Bill Cosby to the Harlem Globetrotters.

Sawgrass Lake Park In St. Petersburg. A forty-acre jungle of lush vegetation surrounding a small lake. The park features a mile-long nature trail and catwalk winding through plant preserves and marsh.

Lake Seminole Park Just northwest of St. Petersburg. Bicycle trails, picnic area, boat launch.

St. Petersburg Beach A beach for doing some serious hanging out.

Fort De Soto County Park You can swim in any of the five small lakes. There's also a wildlife sanctuary. For information, call (813) 866-2484.

Belleair Beach Another nice choice for beachin' between St. Pete and Clearwater beaches. This beach has maybe the whitest sand on the Suncoast. It looks like flour. For information, call (813) 595-4575.

North Shore Park St. Petersburg's 2500-acre public park, with beach, tennis, and baseball diamonds. Call (813) 893-7335.

Treasure Island Beach St. Pete area's cleanest beach, with a four-mile stretch of sugar sand.

For more information, contact:
St. Petersburg Area Chamber of Commerce
401 Third Avenue S.
P.O. Box 1371
St. Petersburg 33731

Sarasota

CHICAGO WHITE SOX

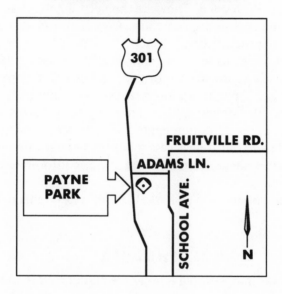

THE TEAM

In 1960, Richard Nixon came *that* close to beating John F. Kennedy in the presidential elections, and a .220 hitter named Carroll Hardy pinch-hit for Ted Williams. Shows you anything can happen. That was also the year the Chicago White Sox moved their spring training camp to Sarasota.

Camp begins in late February at Ed Smith Minor League Complex on 12th Street and Tuttle Avenue. The major league moves camp to Payne Park at the start of the exhibition season.

TEAM HOTEL Sarasota Days Inn, 4900 North Tamiami Trail, Sarasota 33580; (813) 355-9721.

PAYNE PARK One of Florida's old ball yards, this relic's days are numbered. In November 1986, Sarasota voters approved a referendum to provide the White Sox a new spring training complex. The facility will include a 7500-seat stadium at the site of the present Smith Complex.

The new facility will enable the entire organization, including all minor leaguers, to train together. White Sox officials feel the present Payne Park is outmoded. They cite the need for new batting tunnels, concession areas, improved parking, new office and support space, as well as better practice fields.

The team hopes to be in the new facility by spring 1989.

Payne Park is a throwback. For that, and no other reason, it's sad to see it replaced. It retains an air, a mood, that only old ballparks do. As with most Florida parks, there are really no bad seats in the house. When going to an exhibition game at Payne, leave yourself plenty of time to get in and out. The access roads tend to back up, so be patient.

Ticket prices range from $4 to $6.50. For information, call (813) 953-3388.

Address and Phone Payne Park, U.S. 301 and Adams Lane, Sarasota 33580; (813) 957-3910.

THE AREA

The easiest way into Sarasota is on Route 41, but a more scenic approach is via the string of islands across Sarasota Bay. You can island hop on State Road 64 from Bradenton to Anna Maria Island, get on Gulf Drive, and continue through Bradenton Beach and Longboat Key. This will take you to St. Armand's Circle for some breathtaking, very upscale shopping (bring the plastic).

With its superb beaches, many attractions, elegant shops, and thriving arts scene, Sarasota is one of the most exciting vacation spots in the state. And it's easy getting there, either through Sarasota-Bradenton Airport or Tampa International, only fifty-five miles away.

BEDDING DOWN As you would expect in an area like Sarasota, virtually every type of vacation accommodation imaginable is available. As always, make reservations . . . early.

Best Western–Golden Host 4675 Tamiami Trail (U.S. 41), Sarasota; toll free 1-800-528-1234. 80 rooms, lounge, and restaurant. Located one mile south of airport. Beaches six miles away.

Best Western–Royal Palms Motel 1701 North Tamiami Trail (U.S. 41), Sarasota; toll free 1-800-528-1234. 37 rooms, heated pool, close to attractions.

Cabana Inn 2525 South Tamiami Trail (U.S. 41), Sarasota; (813) 955-0195. Spacious rooms, restaurant, lounge. Free coffee every morning.

Days Inn see above under "Team Hotel."

Holiday Inn/Downtown 1 North Tamiami Trail (U.S. 41), Sarasota; (813) 365-1900 or toll free 1-800-HOLIDAY. 100 rooms, dining room. Located on Sarasota Bay, two miles from Lido Beach. Lounge, live entertainment.

Hospitality Inn 1425 South Tamiami Trail, Sarasota; (813) 955-9841. 100 rooms, pool, hot tub, close to shopping, attractions.

Hyatt Sarasota 1000 Boulevard of the Arts, Sarasota; (813) 366-9000 or toll free 1-800-228-9000. 297 rooms, 12 suites, two restaurants, piano bar, gift shop. Minutes from beaches, tennis, and golf.

The Meadows Golf and Tennis Resort 3101 Longmeadow, Sarasota; (813) 378-6660 or toll free 1-800-428-0808. 125 fully furnished villa apartments, with golf course, tennis, dining, shopping.

Pioneer Motel 1188 North Tamiami Trail (U.S. 41), Sarasota; (813) 955-0956. Clean family units and efficiencies, near downtown, beaches, and restaurants.

Sarasota Motor Inn 8150 North Tamiami Trail (U.S. 41), Sarasota; (813) 355-7747. 158 rooms, heated pool, restaurant, lounge, near airport and attractions.

Sundial Motor Inn 4108 North Tamiami Trail (U.S. 41), Sarasota; (813) 351-4910. One mile south of the airport. Efficiencies. Ten minutes to beach.

Tides Inn Motel 1800 Stickney Point Road, Sarasota; (813) 924-7541. One-room fully furnished efficiencies with kitchenettes. Private resort setting, near beaches and shopping.

Travelodge 270 North Tamiami Trail (U.S. 41), Sarasota; (813) 366-0414 or toll free 1-800-255-3050. Near downtown, beaches, and restaurants.

Village des Pins 7964 Timberwood Circle, Sarasota; (813) 923-4966. Decorator furnished, next to Sarasota Square Mall. Private fishing lake.

Harley Sandcastle 1540 Ben Franklin Drive, Lido Key; (813) 388-3941. 179 rooms, many with kitchenettes. Two restaurants, pool, near shopping and golf.

St. Armand's Inn   700 Ben Franklin Drive, Lido Key; (813) 388-2161. Gulf front motel rooms and efficiencies. Heated pool, walk to St. Armand's shopping.

Casa del Mar   4621 Gulf of Mexico Drive, Longboat Key; (813) 383-5549. Lovely two-bedroom, two-bath rental condos. One week minimum.

Longboat Key Club   301 Gulf of Mexico Drive, Longboat Key; (813) 383-8821 or toll free 1-800-237-8821. 221 elegant apartments in a resort setting on gulf. Two eighteen-hole championship courses.

Harbor Towers Yacht & Racquet Club   5855 Midnight Pass Road, Siesta Key; (813) 349-7600 or toll free 1-800-237-4677. 211 luxury condos, one, two, or three bedrooms.

Turtle Beach House   9008 Midnight Pass Road, Siesta Key; (813) 346-1774. Studio, one- and two-bedroom apartments located on Blind Pass near Turtle Beach.

MORSELS   All of the following restaurants are in Sarasota:

El Adobe   4023 South Tamiami Trail (just south of Bee Ridge Road on U.S. 41); (813) 921-7476. Full-menu gourmet Mexican dining.

The Sawmill Restaurant   Crossroads Shopping Center; (813) 366-7292. Beef and seafood. Reservations requested.

House of Chong   6914 South Tamiami Trail; (813) 922-4446. Cantonese dining, with takeout service available.

Oasis Restaurant   3676 Webber Street; (813) 922-6914. Chicken, veal, seafood, full wine service. Reservations requested.

Horsefeathers   1900 Main Street; (813) 366-8088. Cajun, Mexican, pasta, steak, and seafood.

Casa Onesti   3728 North Tamiami Trail; (813) 355-0168. Fine Italian cuisine.

Casa Italia   2080 Constitution Boulevard; (813) 924-1179. Carryout lunches and dinners. Handmade pasta, deli meats.

Shells   7253 South Tamiami Trail; (813) 924-2568. Seafood, shellfish.

Pelican Alley   1009 West Albee Road (just west of U.S. 41); (813) 485-1893. Fresh seafood, hand-cut steaks, on the waterfront. No reservations accepted.

The Melting Pot   1055 South Tamiami Trail (one block east of U.S. 41); (813) 365-2628. Sarasota's only fondue restaurant. A different kind of dining.

Fisherman's Catch   1260 South Tamiami Trail; (813) 966-3832. Seafood.

"SHAKE" IT UP, BABY

Before the White Sox moved to Sarasota, the Boston Red Sox used to train there, in the fifties. Curt Gowdy was the team's play-by-play broadcaster.

One day while going to Payne Park to announce the season's opening exhibition game, Gowdy got caught in traffic, and he was a little late getting into the broadcast booth, sitting down behind the mike just seconds before they went on the air.

He immediately launched into the pregame material—pitching matchups, the weather report, and the like—when he noticed that the mayor of Sarasota was on the field, getting ready to throw out the first ball.

Just then, the late Tommy McCarthy, Boston's legendary press box steward, came into the booth. Tommy had a piece of paper in his hand, and he was asking people in the booth if anybody wanted refreshments. He took the first order and wrote it down on the paper. Gowdy noticed McCarthy, saw the paper in his hand, and glanced at it, thinking McCarthy was supplying him with information for the broadcast.

Gowdy then promptly announced that the first ball of the game would be thrown out by the mayor of Sarasota, Mike Shake. Seems that Gowdy read from McCarthy's first order, which was "milk shake."

Osteria   29½ North Boulevard of the Presidents (above the Bottle Shop on St. Armand's Circle); (813) 388-3671. Northern Italian cuisine.
Café LaChaumière   8197 South Tamiami Trail (across Beneva Road from Sarasota Square Mall); (813) 922-6400. Continental and American cuisine.
Southport   1500 Stickney Point Road; (813) 923-8463. Dining on waterfront. Easy-listening entertainment.
Horn of Plenty   2287 Ringling Boulevard; (813) 953-4335. Six-course international gourmet dinners served in intimate café setting. New menu monthly.
Brenton Reef   3808 North Tamiami Trail; (813) 355-8553. Steak, seafood, prime rib. Complimentary hors d'oeuvres.
The Bijou Café   Corner of First and Pineapple in downtown area; (813) 366-8111. American and continental dinners.

ATTRACTIONS
The John and Mable Ringling Museum of Art   This is the state's official museum of art, housing one of the nation's most dazzling displays of Baroque art. Rubens, Rembrandt, and other masters are featured. The Circus Gallery houses a colorful collection of memorabilia, including parade wagons, calliopes, costumes, and posters. Located off U.S. 41, two miles north of downtown Sarasota. Information: (813) 355-5101.
Bellm Cars & Music of Yesterday   An outstanding collection of fully restored antique autos, from Rolls Royces to Pierce Arrows. Other displays include 1200 music boxes and 250 antique arcade games. Open seven days a week on 5500 North U.S. 41. Information: (813) 355-6228.
Sarasota Jungle Gardens   Sixteen acres of jungle and formal gardens. Kids will enjoy the petting zoo. Two blocks west of U.S. 41, two miles north of the Sarasota bayfront. Information: (813) 355-5305.
Jungle Gardens' Reptile World   Live snakes, turtles, and other things slithery, featured in five shows daily. This attraction is included in your admission to Jungle Gardens.
Lionel Train & Shell Museum   The museum displays hundreds of model trains and antique gauge sets. Some trains can be run by visitors. A coral reef, exotic sea life, and sea shells are also displayed. Located on U.S. 41 across from Sarasota-Bradenton Airport and open every day from 9:00 A.M. to 5:00 P.M. Information: (813) 355-8184.
Le Barge   This cruise on Sarasota's Intracoastal Waterway is both relaxing and educational. Narrated tours highlight city landmarks and points of history. Information: (813) 366-6116.

Spanish Point at the Oaks   Thirty-acre spread of environmental, archaeological, and historic sites, located on Little Sarasota Bay in Osprey. Information: (813) 966-5214.

Mote Marine Science Center   Live sharks, living seagrass, rays, and other animals make this a popular spot. The shell collection is spectacular. Located at 1600 City Island Park. Open daily except Monday. Information: (813) 388-2451.

Warm Mineral Springs   Experience the regenerative powers of a mud bath, without your mother yelling at you! The natural warm springs are eighty-seven degrees Fahrenheit. Use exit 34 off I-75 (south Sarasota County). Information: (813) 426-1692.

Asolo State Theater   This spectacular eighteenth-century building was imported whole from Asolo, Italy (twenty miles from Venice), and installed at the Ringling Museum of Art, just off North U.S. 41. Maybe the best professional theater in Florida. Call (813) 355-5137.

Van Wezel Hall   The architectural landmark on Sarasota's bayfront, the building is visible from miles away. Shows include the symphony, jazz concerts, opera, ballet, and choral productions. Located at 777 North Tamiami Trail; (813) 953-3366.

Theater of the Arts   Sarasota's opera company, at 61 North Pineapple Avenue, noted for its high standards and performances; (813) 366-8450.

St. Armand's Circle   State Road 780, Sarasota; (813) 388-1554. This circle of upscale boutiques and restaurants form a ring around a beautiful garden. The expensive shops, great art galleries, and superb dining draw visitors from all over the state.

Sarasota Square Mall   Located at 8201 South Tamiami Trail about eight miles south of the city. Stores include Sears, J. C. Penney, and Maas Brothers; (813) 922-9609.

Bobby Jones Golf Club   1000 Circus Boulevard; (813) 955-8041. Thirty-six holes, par 72.

Forest Lake Golf Club   2401 Beneva Road; (813) 922-1312. Eighteen-hole, championship course, putting greens.

Rolling Green Golf Club   4501 North Tuttle Avenue; (813) 355-7621. Eighteen holes, par 72. Driving range.

Sarasota Golf Club   7280 North Leewynn Drive (three-quarters of a mile east of I-75 off Bee Ridge Road); (813) 371-2431. Full facilities, including driving range and chipping green.

Village Green Golf Course   3500 Pembrook Drive; (813) 922-9500. Eighteen-hole, executive-length course. Teaching pro.

There are numerous tennis courts in Sarasota, ranging from free municipal courts to private tennis clubs, plus those at hotels and motels. Call the Sarasota Tourism Association for a complete listing of tennis courts.

Chances to indulge in boating and fishing are outstanding, since Sarasota is linked to the Gulf of Mexico by inlets. There are also Sarasota Bay, the Intracoastal Waterway, and the gulf itself, as well as a number of freshwater lakes. Boat ramps are located at the Civic Center complex downtown, on City Island north of Lido Key, and at Turtle Beach on southern Siesta Key. The following marinas operate boat rental and charter businesses:

Cannon's Marina   6060 Gulf of Mexico Drive, Longboat Key; (813) 383-3252.

Marina Jack   Marina Plaza Bayfront, Sarasota; (813) 365-4232.

Siesta Key Marina   1265 Stickney Point Road, Sarasota; (813) 349-8880.

> For more information, contact:
> **Sarasota Tourism Association**
> **655 North Tamiami Trail**
> **Sarasota 33577**
> **(813) 957-1877**

Tampa

CINCINNATI REDS

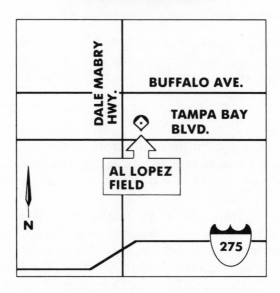

THE TEAM

With the exception of the World War II years of 1943 through 1945, the Reds have trained in Tampa continuously since 1931. During the war, travel restrictions were placed on all baseball teams, and the Reds trained on the campus of Indiana University in Bloomington.

The Reds' long relationship with Tampa has been a little shaky in recent years. The Reds were talking to some folks at nearby Plant City, and for a while, it looked as if a deal was in the works. Behind-the-scenes talks may still be going on, judging by the noncommittal statements made by both the ball club and the town. But, for the time being anyhow, it looks as if the Reds will stay in Tampa.

REDSLAND Camp opens for batterymen usually around February 21, with the full squad reporting by the end of the month. Workouts are held at Redsland until the opening of the grapefruit league schedule, usually around March 6 or 7. At that time, the major league roster moves to Al Lopez Field.

Address and Phone Redsland, Himes Street and Columbus Avenue, Tampa 33677; (813) 874-0253.

TEAM HOTEL Howard Johnson Plaza, 700 North Westshore Boulevard, Tampa; (813) 873-7900.

AL LOPEZ FIELD Another of the "taste of baseball" parks, Al Lopez Field is a delightful place for watching a ball game. Beyond the left field fence, you see the football stadium, but it's not a distraction . . . just a point of character.

Though the stadium itself has all the classic earmarks of spring training baseball—the easy accessibility of players, the close proximity of stands to fields, a general flavor of informality—keep in mind that Al Lopez Field is located in a busy, large city. The baseball experience in Tampa is relaxing, but in a different way than, say, Dunedin or Clearwater.

Tampa's a big town, with all its benefits and hassles. There's lots of traffic going over the major highways of I-275, I-75, and I-4, and it can be confusing to find your way around—so make sure you know where you're going when you drive to Al Lopez. The most direct way to the stadium is to take I-275 to the Dale Mabry Highway exit. Take Dale Mabry north to Tampa Bay Boulevard. The stadium is at that intersection.

Game time at Al Lang Field is 1:00 P.M. Ticket prices range from $4 to $6. Check for senior citizen discounts. Call the ticket office at the number listed below.

Address and Phone Al Lopez Field, Dale Mabry and Tampa Bay Boulevard, P.O. Box 4648, Tampa 33677; (813) 873-8617.

THE AREA

Sometimes, even the most obvious things are the most obscure. There's the story of Jerry Willard, a catcher with the Indians, who was suffering from a sore throat. When the trainer told him to gargle with warm water, he asked: "Where do you buy that stuff?"

Which brings us to an obvious, yet sometimes overlooked, point about Tampa—that it's one of the most lively, upbeat, and trendy cities in the country.

As we said before, Tampa is a big city (300,000 people), and not without its problems. There are no great beaches. It's crowded. Tampa Bay is the country's seventh busiest port, moving well over 50 million tons of cargo each year. All the business, however, has left the bay polluted in areas.

A large part of the city has a blue-collar backbone: workers in cigar factories (3 million ropes a day rolling out of Ybor City) and beer breweries, and laborers packing seafood and harvesting strawberries. But an explosive building of office space has led to an immigration of lawyers, businessmen, and other yuppie types.

BEDDING DOWN   Tampa has more than fifty top quality hotels, with some 12,000 rooms. Here are a few, all in Tampa itself:

Harbour Island Hotel   725 South Harbour Island Boulevard; (813) 229-5000 or toll free 1-800-228-0808. More than 300 elegant rooms and suites, restaurant, guest privileges at the Athletic Club.

Hyatt Regency Westshore   6200 Courtney Campbell Causeway; (813) 874-1234 or toll free 1-800-228-9000. Private beach, luxury rooms.

Hyatt Regency Tampa   Two Tampa City Center; (813) 225-1234 or toll free 1-800-228-9000. Downtown location, superb dining and accommodations.

Embassy Suites   4400 West Cypress Street; (813) 873-8675 or toll free 1-800-EMBASSY. Minutes from Tampa airport. All rooms are luxurious suites, with free breakfast every morning. Pool, Jacuzzi.

Bay Harbour Inn   7700 Courtney Campbell Causeway; (813) 885-2541 or toll free (800) 237-7773. Tampa's only luxury beachfront hotel. Free limo to the airport. Restaurant and lounge. Owned by George Steinbrenner.

Tampa Hilton   200 North Ashley; (813) 223-2222. Convenient downtown location, minutes from Busch Gardens.

Sabal Park Holiday Inn   10315 East Buffalo Avenue at I-75; (813) 623-6363. 265 rooms, 36 executive suites, 5 penthouse suites, two restaurants, nightclub, tennis.

The Residence Inn   3075 North Rocky Point Drive; (813) 887-5576 or toll free 1-800-331-3131. Fully furnished suites, complimentary breakfast and airport limo.

Holiday Inn/Airport   4500 West Cypress Street; (813) 879-4800. Five minutes from airport and Al Lopez Field. 500 rooms, 23 suites, fitness center, dining, entertainment.

Admiral Benbow Inn   1200 North Westshore Boulevard; toll free 1-800-237-7535. 240 rooms, restaurant, lounge, health club, pool.

Hall of Fame Golf & Tennis Resort   222 North Westshore Boulevard; (813) 877-1600 or toll free 1-800-237-3801. 185 rooms, free golf and tennis, restaurant, lounge.

Guest Quarters Hotel   555 North Westshore Boulevard; toll free 1-800-424-2900. 221 rooms, restaurant, lounge, full service.

Howard Johnson Plaza Hotel   700 North Westshore Boulevard; toll free 1-800-654-2000. 280 rooms, valet service, restaurant, health club, entertainment.

Ramada Inn   4139 East Busch Boulevard; toll free 1-800-2RAMADA. 260 rooms, restaurant, tennis, entertainment.

Sheraton Tampa East   7401 East Hillsborough Avenue; (813) 626-0999. 156 rooms, valet service, restaurant, lounge.

Tampa Marriott Westshore   1001 North Westshore Boulevard; toll free 1-800-228-9290. 312 rooms, with full hotel services.

MORSELS   Tampa restaurants appeal to a rainbow of tastes; you'll find Spanish, Italian, French, Chinese, Mexican, and just good country cooking. All these places are in Tampa:

Bern's Steak House   1208 South Howard Avenue; (813) 251-2421. Great selection of beef and wines. Steak is aged up to eight weeks. But the mind-boggling part of this restaurant is the wine cellar, with its half million bottles representing over 6000 varieties! One note: if you intend to order the Gruaud-Larose 1833, take about $4100 extra with you . . . excluding tip, of course.

Backstage Restaurant   Ashley Plaza Hotel, 111 West Fortune Street; (813) 223-1351. Chicken, black angus steaks, and four-pound Maine lobsters.

Galerie Restaurant   Pickett Suite Hotel, 3050 North Rocky Point Drive W.; (813) 888-8800. Casual dining with a varied menu.

The Island Room Restaurant   Harbour Island Hotel, 725 Harbour Island Boulevard; (813) 229-5000. Seafood, Wisconsin veal, caviar, and local vegetables in classical French cuisine.

Verandah   5250 West Kennedy Boulevard; (813) 876-0168. Fresh seafood, beef, veal, and poultry in an elegant southern Victorian setting.

A TOUCH OF GREATNESS

My first year of spring training was in 1954 with the Cleveland Indians, a team that won 111 games and lost 43, which is a record that stands to this day. In that season, Casey Stengel won 103 games, the most he ever won as a big-league manager. Yet he finished eight games out.

"Like any rookie that goes to camp—be it player, broadcaster, or writer—I was in awe of some of the people I met, even though, for the two previous years, I had been broadcasting Cleveland Browns football. Nevertheless, it was a matter of being young and nervous with the baseball players, who—as a general rule—are not quite as easy to get to know as football players because they are exposed to the public on almost a daily basis. This came as a surprise to me.

"In the fifties, there was not as much individual instruction in a spring training camp as you get today. Rookies and veterans also were completely stratified, unlike today, where all players on the team are usually friendly with each other. Back then, a veteran looked on a rookie as a guy after his job. Today, with contracts being what they are, this threat is less obvious.

"As you go through generations of baseball teams, as I have, it is not all that uncommon for one generation to think it was better than the succeeding one. When players from 1954 get together in 1964, they say 'These kids don't have the desire we had.' When the 1964 guys look at the 1974 guys, they say the same thing. And in '84 they say the same thing. It's just that, when they were there, players remember how hungry they were, and how much they wanted to be in the big leagues. That never changes. Players today are just as hungry."
—Ken Coleman

Chuck's Steak House 11911 North Dale Mabry; (813) 962-2226. Aged steaks, with extensive salad bar and wine menu.

Oyster's Seafaring Pub & Restaurant 13731 North Dale Mabry; (813) 960-0930. Fresh seafood, with a selection of forty beers.

Yankee Trader Restaurant Bay Harbour Inn, 7700 Courtney Campbell Causeway; (813) 885-2541. Specializes in fresh seafood, prime rib, and steaks.

Emmy's Family Restaurant 3120 West Hillsborough; (813) 874-3950. Family-style dining.

Silver Ring Café 1831 East Seventh Avenue; (813) 248-2549. Cuban cuisine.

Armani's At Hyatt Westshore, 6200 Courtney Campbell Causeway; (813) 874-1234. Rooftop restaurant featuring northern Italian cuisine.

Lorenzo's Italian Restaurant 3615 West Humphrey; (813) 932-6641. Fine Italian menu.

Mama Mia Ristorante At Holiday Inn, 4732 North Dale Mabry; (813) 877-6061. Dine in an authentic recreation of an Italian village. Wine and antipasto free with dinners.

Columbia Restaurant 2117 East Seventh Avenue, in the Ybor City section of Tampa; (813) 248-4961. Fine Spanish dining.

Café de Paris 4430 West Kennedy Boulevard; (813) 876-5422. French cuisine.

Casa Gallardo 13001 North Dale Mabry; (813) 963-1857. Mexican fare.

Lupton's Fat Man's Barbeque 5299 East Busch Boulevard; (813) 985-6963. Authentic Southern cooking about a half mile from Busch Gardens.

Kaori Bana 13180 North Dale Mabry Highway; (813) 968-3801. Japanese cooking.

Mai King 8503 West Hillsborough Avenue; (813) 885-4125. Chinese menu.

Malio's Café 301 South Dale Mabry Highway; (813) 879-3233. Casual dining, and a great sports hangout.

Matterhorn Hofbrau Haus 810 East Skagway; (813) 932-0780. German cuisine.

ATTRACTIONS Let it all hang out when you're not at the ballpark.

Ybor City This is the historic Latin Quarter of Tampa. The area is a bundling of parks, theaters, clubs, museums, and restaurants. Street vendors sell their crabs, coffee, and cigars. Recent restoration efforts are bringing back a vitality and freshness. Heart of the area is 12th to 22nd streets between Seventh and Palm avenues.

Busch Gardens Busch Boulevard; (813) 988-5171. The Dark Continent adventure draws visitors from across the country. Rides, entertainment, games, and a huge zoo, inspired by African themes. Six miles northeast of downtown.

Adventure Island 4545 Bougainvillea Avenue; (813) 971-7978. A thirteen-acre water theme park featuring slides, pools, beaches, waterfalls, and man-made waves.

The Market on Harbour Island 601 Harbour Island Boulevard; (813) 229-5080. A marketplace featuring fifty retail shops, twenty-two eateries, two sit-down restaurants, and boat cruises.

Museum of Science of Industry 4801 East Fowler Avenue; (813) 985-5531. A hands-on museum that involves visitors. You can get caught in a hurricane, go up against computers and more in the interactive displays.

Seminole Cultural Center 5221 North Orient Road; (813) 623-3549. Fascinating Seminole village, housing the world's only Seminole museum. Alligator wrestling, snake demonstrations.

Tampa Museum of Art 601 Doyle Carlton Drive; (813) 223-8130. Six galleries include everything from Calder mobiles to Greek pottery to impressionist masterpieces. Lectures, films, and art classes are also featured.

H. B. Plant Museum 401 West Kennedy Boulevard; (813) 253-3333. This museum was, when built in 1899, the plush Tampa Bay Hotel. It cost railroad tycoon Henry B. Plant the unheard of sum of $3.5 million to build. The museum houses permanent exhibitions of European and Oriental furnishings and art objects.

Lowry Park Zoo 7525 North Boulevard; (813) 223-8271. Natural habitats and wooden walkways make this more than just another zoo. Kids will love the Storeybook Park, featuring life-size Little Red Riding Hood, Snow White, and others.

Tampa Bay Performing Arts Center A magnificent arts complex, including three theaters. Call (813) 229-7827 for complete information.

Tampa Theater One of the great, old movie palaces restored to its 1926 perfection. Located on Franklin Street, this theater offers a selection of films and concerts.

The list of things to do goes on and on. For sports, try Tampa Greyhound Dog Track, (813) 932-4313; Tampa Jai-Alai, (813) 831-1411; and East Bay Raceway (auto racing), (813) 677-RACE. Participant sports include boating, fishing, golf, and tennis. Call the visitors association for details.

Oh, yeah, all you voyeurs, don't forget the strip joints located on Dale Mabry Highway.

For more information, contact:
Tampa/Hillsborough Convention and Visitors Association
100 South Ashley Drive, Suite 850
P.O. Box 519
Tampa 33601
(813) 223-1111

Baseball City

KANSAS CITY ROYALS

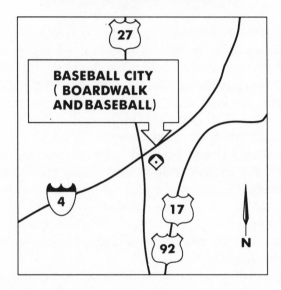

THE TEAM

Ask Uncle McNally for his map of Florida (you know, Uncle Rand), and find the intersection of Interstate 4 and U.S. Highway 27. Now look for Baseball City. Now stop looking, because you won't find it.

Baseball City is the name for the unincorporated 135-acre site of Boardwalk and Baseball, twenty-five minutes southwest of Orlando. The former site of Circus World was reborn in 1987 as a major league theme park, competing for tourist bucks with Walt Disney's Magic Kingdom, EPCOT Center, and Sea World. The Royals opened their camp at Baseball City for the first time in 1988.

The concept behind the park is the combination of two classic American entertainment traditions: baseball and a Coney Island–style amusement park. About $50 million has been poured into the site, including all the preparations needed to draw the Royals from Ft. Meyers, their only spring home since the club's inception in 1969.

TEAM HOTEL   The Royals have made no decision on a team hotel going into 1988. For information on where the Royals will be staying, contact the club in Kansas City: Kansas City Royals, P.O. Box 419969, One Royals Way, Kansas City, MO 64141; (816) 921-8000.

BASEBALL CITY   The Royals signed a ten-year lease with Boardwalk and Baseball beginning in 1988. The complex includes a sixty-five-hundred-seat stadium where the Royals will play their home games for the grapefruit league schedule. The stadium includes a "Stadium Club" type restaurant, of a kind found in some major league ball parks. The restaurant is situated so that fans can eat and watch the game. Five other practice diamonds are located beyond the stadium fences, including a four-diamond cluster centered by an observation tower.

To construct the six diamonds, workers bulldozed 1 million tons of earth and rubble: the site of the playing fields used to be the dump for Circus World, the site's previous attraction. And you've heard about the ups and downs of baseball? While the diamonds are level, there can be a twenty-foot difference from field to field because of the grading that had to be done.

The facilities will house both the forty-man major league roster, as well as the entire minor league system. The Royals entry in the A-level Florida State League will play their home games at the stadium.

The Royals will join the county's two other teams—the Red Sox (Winter Haven) and the Tigers (Lakeland)—in competing for the somewhat coveted Polk County Trophy, awarded to the team with the best record in head-to-head play.

While the Royals are the main baseball attraction, visitors should make sure they visit "A Taste of Cooperstown," a 1000-square-foot showcase of memorabilia provided by the National Baseball Hall of Fame in Cooperstown, New York. The Hall of Fame only rarely makes loans of any consequence, and this exhibit is one of the largest ever to leave Cooperstown.

More than one hundred artifacts are on display. These include uniforms, caps, bats, autographed baseballs, spikes, gloves, equipment, scorecards, tickets, photos, bubble-gum cards, and more. The emphasis is on Hall of Famers, with memorabilia from Babe Ruth, Lou Gehrig, Mel Ott, Ted Williams, Willie Mays, Warren Spahn, Stan Musial, Al Kaline, and Hank Aaron. Recent stars include Pete Rose, Carl Yastrzemski, Steve Carlton, and Tom Seaver. Also exhibited is a locker from the Yankee Stadium clubhouse dating back to the time of Ruth. One of Ruth's jerseys (size 46) from 1929 to 1934 is also displayed.

Tickets for Royals ball games can be purchased as part of an admission ticket to the overall park, or separately.

Address and Phone   Boardwalk and Baseball, P.O. Box 800, Orlando 32802; (305) 422-0643 or (813) 424-2421.

THE REST OF THE PARK   The great thing about Boardwalk and Baseball is that, in one location, there's something for everyone in the family . . . even those who aren't baseball fans. Even without the Royals, the amusement park itself is quite an attraction. Park hours are 9:00 A.M. to 10:00 P.M. Sunday through Thursday, and 9:00 A.M. to midnight on weekends. A tram will take you from the parking lot to the main gate.

For the young, the young at heart, and anyone else with a lead stomach, there are thirty rides, including the Florida Hurricane, one of the longest wooden roller coaster rides in the country. If you want to sit it out while the kids are riding the Monster (don't ask) for the seventh time, you can do so under the shade of the trees at the Oasis. The streams and reflecting pools offer a restful haven.

Other park highlights you'll enjoy are the following:

Colorado Riders   This forty-minute show is a trip through Colorado during the gold-rush days. The presentation features original sets and music, a cast of thirty actors, and stunt riders. The 2500-seat covered theater lets you enjoy the show out of the weather. Replica wagons, including stagecoaches, were built from authentic plans.

Boardwalk Theatre   Walk inside, and you're hit with a six-story-high movie screen. The film explores one of nature's great wonders in *Grand Canyon: The Hidden Secrets*. It's a half-hour round-screen flick that plunges you into the middle of mile-deep gorges. Great drama-mine.

Professor Bubble's Magical Factory   Kids and magic . . . when does that combination ever fail? Animal balloons are turned into life-size characters, mushrooms transform into chocolate chip cookies. The kids will be enthralled.

The Boardwalk   The inlaid, mile-long boardwalk replaces the concrete pathways of Circus World, the site's previous attraction. Besides looking nice, the boardwalk eliminates the heat-radiating stone walkways, keeping guests cooler. The boardwalk connects the park's shows and rides. Along the boardwalk, you'll find lots of entertainment, with jugglers, dancers, and musicians. The wood itself deserves a note. It's jarrah timber, from western Australia. Jarrah is native to Australia, where the government farms 4 million acres of timber. It's an extremely dense wood that's expected to last fifty years with no chemical or varnishing treatment.

The Midway   A midway is a midway is a midway, and you'll find what you'd expect here, from skee ball to ring toss. There are batting cages and other baseball-themed participation events.

Dancing, USA   This facility features professional dancers. When the dance team isn't on the floor, the Boardwalk deejay will play requests ranging from Tommy Dorsey to Bruce Springsteen (maybe even Twisted Sister).

The park is shaded by more than 2500 trees, beautifully landscaped and affording welcome shade.

Eateries   You'll find plenty to wolf down at Boardwalk and Baseball. Besides the stadium restaurant is Colorado Barbecue, with the flavors of the Old West. Other sit-down restaurants include Salerno Express, housed in a refurbished railroad car; San Antone, with Mexican cuisine; and Chicken 'n Biscuit, with Southern cooking. There are food stands throughout the park.

BEDDING DOWN   The acreage surrounding Boardwalk and Baseball is undergoing furious development, and that includes the construction of hotel space. For example, a Day's Inn Motel is being constructed in Baseball City. Others are in the works. So with new hotel space being added regularly, the best thing to do is contact the Boardwalk and Baseball public relations office for complete and up-to-date listings. You might also want to consider staying in the nearby Orlando (Twins) or Kissimmee (Astros) areas. See the entries in this book for listings there.

You also can try accommodations in the nearby communities of Haines City, Davenport, and Lake Alfred:

Holiday Inn   U.S. 17 and I-4, Haines City; (813) 424-2211 or toll free 1-800-238-8000. Located right across from Boardwalk and Baseball.

Haines City Motel   1010 East Hinton Avenue, Haines City; (813) 442-1251. Singles, doubles, and family rooms, pool. Eleven miles from Baseball City.

Best Western U.S. 27 at I-4 North, Davenport; (813) 424-2511. Just minutes from Baseball City. 158 rooms, pool, restaurant, lounge. Close to an eighteen-hole golf course.

Chalet Suzanne P.O. Drawer AC, Lake Alfred; (813) 676-1477.

Holiday Motel and Apartments 801 Hinson Avenue, Haines City; (813) 422-1293. Rooms and furnished apartments. Close to restaurants.

Howard Johnson's Motel and Restaurant U.S. 27 at I-4 North, Davenport; (813) 424-2311.

John's Resort Motel and Restaurant 1504 U.S. 27, Haines City; (813) 422-8621.

Port Hatchineha Motel 21020 Hatchineha Road, Haines City; (813) 439-2376.

State Motel 905 U.S. 27 North, Haines City; (813) 422-1331.

MORSELS As we mentioned earlier, you'll find plenty of eating places at Baseball City. Again, as with hotel space, new restaurants are expected to follow the development of the Baseball City area. Contact the Haines City Chamber of Commerce for a complete listing of area restaurants. You can write to them at P.O. Box 986, U.S. 27 North, Haines City 33844; (813) 422-3751.

You can also make the twenty-five-minute journey to Orlando and find a world of eating experiences (see the restaurants listed in the Orlando section of this book). U.S. Highways 27 and 17/92 are loaded with fast-food restaurants. In Haines City, try the following:

Bojangles 701 Hinson Avenue; (813) 422-3255. Varied menu.

Golden Corral 608 U.S. 27 North; (813) 422-7117. Family-style restaurant featuring steaks and salad bar.

STAY TUNED FOR FURTHER DEVELOPMENTS In the next few years, the area surrounding Baseball City will be undergoing a complete transformation. High-rise hotels, shopping malls, restaurants, condos, resorts, housing and more are being built, or are on the drawing boards.

In the next ten years, developers will drop hundreds of millions of dollars into the area. One example is the Deer Creek Golf and Tennis Resort being built on 650 acres of land surrounding Boardwalk and Baseball. This facility will include an eighteen-hole course, clubhouse, multifamily housing, businesses, and space for more than 1100 recreational vehicles. A nine-acre piece of road-front land adjacent to the Deer Creek development sold in March 1987 for $650,000 . . . about

THE MAKINGS OF A THEME PARK

To make Boardwalk and Baseball what it is, some Herculean logistics were needed. Here's a look at some interesting (and obscure) facts.

Board by it all—to make the boardwalk, aluminum framing was laid for 35,000 2" by 4" jarrah boards, each 14½ feet long. If stretched end to end, the lumber for the walkway would extend ninety-six miles, or about the distance from Orlando to St. Petersburg. Because jarrah is so dense, the lumber is installed using flat-head screws . . . 423,360 screws, to be exact. The 425,000 feet of wood cost $1.3 million. It is expected to last fifty years without any chemical treatment. The Australian wood is red when alive and sunbleaches to a gray color. The timbers were purchased from Bunnings, Ltd., Australia's largest timber producer. The entire shipment traveled from Perth through the Panama Canal to Charleston, South Carolina, before being sent to Boardwalk and Baseball via truck.

Water, water everywhere—the lagoon for the log flume ride (a four-minute ride that empties into a midpark lake) holds about 1 million gallons of water. Its three pumps can move 23,000 gallons a minute. Even at that rate, it took two days to fill the lagoon. If park employees had used standard three-quarter-inch garden hose (the kind you use to water the lawn), it would take about 2842 hours—118 days—to fill it up.

They build horses, don't they?—the carousel in the center of the park is also special. The fiberglass horses are made to look like the famliar wooden horses hand carved at the turn of the century, horses that populate the same spot in the American psyche that a ball game under a summer sun occupies. All the horses on the thirty-six-foot diameter wheel are "jumpers," that is, horses posed with curled legs, going up and down. This is unusual; the outside horses on a carousel are traditionally "standers"—straight legs with no movement up or down. Just in case you were wondering, an antique carousel in reasonably good shape will sell for about $40,000. "Gee, Wilbur. . . ."

$74,000 an acre (for land assessed for tax purposes at about $10,000 an acre). And that's just the beginning. One developer says that to get anyone's attention today, you'd have to come up with $150,000 to $170,000 an acre; land fronting U.S. 27 could go as high as $300,000 an acre. People are actually pulling property off the market until the full value of the land is realized.

This kind of development can be a boom to the local economies, but also a Frankenstein monster that turns on its creators. Overdeveloped land can have serious consequences on the aesthetic and environmental appeal that for so long has made Florida unique. Visitors can only take so much, spend so much, do so many things, and—unless it proceeds in a responsible and well-thought-out way—development will lead to a survival of the fittest among Florida attractions, and the areas that host them.

ATTRACTIONS Baseball City may be all the attraction you'll need to know. The baseball is great, the amusements just as good, and there's something for everyone, for all interests and all ages. For the real action, elsewhere and nearby, explore the Orlando area. You can also go south a short way to Winter Haven or travel the few miles east to Kissimmee (check listings in this book for attractions).

Baseball City is almost literally the heart of Florida—nearly equidistant from Jacksonville and Miami north and south, and from Tampa and Melbourne west and east. As such, it is, along with the other Central Florida towns in this section, a fine vacation base from which to explore the rest of Florida.

Haines City has three sizable shopping centers, in addition to a number of "strip" businesses along highways.

The area has numerous lakes for fishing and boating. There are several fishing camps in the Haines City area. Most local lakes have boat ramps. Lakes Lowry, Hamilton, Marion, Pierce, Hatchineha, and Hammock are noted for their bass, where ten- to thirteen-pounders can be caught.

The more than fifteen golf courses in the area include:

Grenelefe Golf and Tennis Resort   3200 State Road 546, Haines City; (813) 422-7511. This is a private course, but the golf studio is open to the public.

Poinciana Golf and Racquet Club   500 East Cypress Parkway, Poinciana; (305) 348-5000.

Sun Air Country Club   Route 1, Watkins Road, Haines City; (813) 439-1756. Public.

Tennis courts are located in nearby communities. Other recreational activities around the Baseball City area are sightseeing, camping, hunting, square dancing, and various cultural events.

> For more information, contact:
> **Haines City Chamber of Commerce**
> **P.O. Box 986**
> **U.S. Highway 27 North**
> **Haines City 33844**
> **(813) 422-3751**

Kissimmee

HOUSTON ASTROS

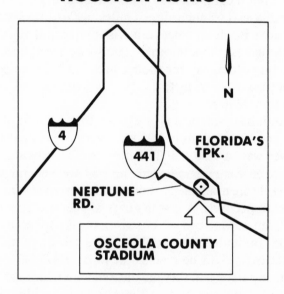

THE TEAM

The Astros complex is almost beyond modern . . . it's where the Jetsons will be playing baseball in a few hundred years. Well, that's how it seems, anyway, especially compared to the club's old facilities in Cocoa, which resembled trappings of the China-Burma Theater of World War II. Houston said goodbye to Cocoa in 1985, when they began training in Kissimmee.

TEAM HOTEL   Fantasy Club Villas, 2935 Hart Avenue, Kissimmee 32741; (305) 396-1808.

OSCEOLA STADIUM   This 5200-seat stadium is one of Florida's best. It's comfortable, well designed with the fan in mind, and an intelligent parking situation makes getting in and out no harder than it has to be. The field is expertly and beautifully manicured. Simply put, you're going to enjoy this ballyard.

Beyond the left field fence is a four-diamond complex with a command post hub in the center, housing clubhouses and observation areas. These fields, too, are well placed and "fan-friendly." The stadium also is home turf for the Osceola Astros, the franchise's Class A Florida State League entry.

The $5.5 million complex is situated on an eighty-acre site one mile west of turnpike exit 65 and thirteen miles east of Interstate 4, off U.S. 192 on Osceola Boulevard between Kissimmee and St. Cloud.

The clubhouse is a mammoth 30,000 square feet, containing club offices, meeting rooms, locker rooms, and dining facilities. When the Astros aren't using it, in fact, the facility gets booked as a meeting and convention center.

The exhibition season begins late in the first week of March. Game time at the county stadium is 1:05 P.M., with occasional night games getting under way at 7:30 P.M. Ticket prices for individual games are $6 for boxes, $5 for reserved seats, and $4 for general admission.

Season tickets are available for boxes and reserved seating, with prices $102 and $85 respectively. A season's pass will get you into the seventeen or so home games. Mail orders for season tickets are accepted through December 15. Individual game tickets go on sale on or about January 5. The ticket office can be reached at (305) 933-5400.

Astro officials have said they are pleased with their relationship with Osceola County and are hoping that the relationship develops even further, along the lines of, say, the Dodgers and Vero Beach. With the increasing competitiveness among Florida areas for big-league teams, that remains to be seen. You never know when a town will come along with an offer that can't be refused. But given the fact that the Astros have one of the top facilities in Florida, they will probably be there for a while.

Address and Phone   Osceola County Stadium, 1000 Osceola Boulevard, Kissimmee 32741. (305) 933-2520 or 933-6500.

THE AREA

The Kissimmee/St. Cloud resort area is without question one of the world's top resort areas, not so much for what it has to offer, but more for what it's near. It's just fifteen miles east of Walt Disney World and is centrally located among such attractions as Sea World, Boardwalk and Baseball, Cypress Gardens, Kennedy Space Center, and Busch Gardens.

The area includes about 17,000 hotel rooms, 5000 campsites and 120 restaurants, with more being built every year. Accessibility is not a problem, with the Orlando International Airport only twenty-five minutes away.

BEDDING DOWN   The ever-growing number of hotel and motel rooms in the Kissimmee/St. Cloud area has kept prices stable. Double occupancy rooms begin at about $40 at smaller motels, and $60 at larger properties. The Kissimmee/St. Cloud Convention and Visitors Bureau offers a detailed list of all hotels and motels in the area. Write for it . . . it's free. Here's a partial listing of properties. All are in Kissimmee. All feature restaurants, pools, and other niceties. Call each place for detailed information and rates.

Best Western Vacation Lodge   8600 West Highway 192; (305) 396-0100 or toll free 1-800-327-9151.

Chalet Motel   4741 West Highway 192; (305) 393-1677.

Comfort Inn East   402 Simpson Road; (305) 846-1530 or toll free 1-800-228-5150.

Days Inn Main Gate   5840 West Highway 192; (305) 396-7969 or toll free 1-800-327-9126.

Days Inn of Kissimmee   2095 East Highway 192; (305) 846-7136 or toll free 1-800-325-2525.

Econo Lodge Main Gate East   6051 West Highway 192; (305) 396-1748 or toll free 1-800-654-7160.

Econo Lodge Main Gate West   8260 West Highway 192; (305) 396-9300 or toll free 1-800-327-9077.

Fantasy Club Villas   2935 Hart Avenue (West Highway 192); (305) 396-1808 or toll free 1-800-874-8047.

Gala Vista Motor Inn   5995 West Highway 192; (305) 396-4300 or toll free 1-800-223-1584.

Hilton Inn Gateway   7470 West Highway 192; (305) 396-4400 or toll free 1-800-327-9170.

Holiday Inn Kissimmee/Exit 65   2145 East Highway 192; (305) 846-4646 or toll free 1-800-HOLIDAY.

Holiday Inn Main Gate West   7300 West Highway 192; (305) 396-7300 or toll free 1-800-HOLIDAY.

Howard Johnson Motor Lodge 2323 East Highway 192; (305) 846-4900 or toll free 1-800-654-2000.

Hyatt 6375 West Highway 192; (305) 396-1234 or toll free 1-800-228-9000.

Kon-Tiki Master Hosts Resort 7514 West Highway 192; (305) 396-2000 or toll free 1-800-327-9175.

Master Hosts Inn/Cedar Lakeside 4960 West Highway 192; (305) 396-1376 or toll free 1-800-327-0072.

Ramada Inn Kissimmee East 2050 East Highway 192; (305) 846-4545 or toll free 1-800-327-6908.

Ramada Resort Main Gate 2950 Reedy Creek Boulevard; (305) 396-4466 or toll free 1-800-327-9127.

Red Carpet Inn East 4700 West Highway 192; (305) 396-1133 or toll free 1-800-874-1156.

Regency Inn 8660 West Highway 192; (305) 396-4500 or toll free 1-800-327-9129.

Sheraton Lakeside Inn 7711 West Highway 192; (305) 396-2222 or toll free 1-800-325-3535.

Stagecoach Resort Inn 4311 West Highway 192; (305) 396-4213 or toll free 1-800-327-9155.

TraveLodge Kissimmee Flags 2407 West Highway 192; (305) 933-2400 or toll free 1-800-352-4725.

TraveLodge Main Gate East 5711 West Highway 192; (305) 396-4222 or toll free 1-800-327-1128.

Wilson World Hotel 7491 West Highway 192; (305) 396-6000 or toll free 1-800-327-0049.

MORSELS Dining is an important part of any vacation, and in the Kissimmee area, you'll find a wide variety of restaurants to choose from. A complete listing is available from the convention and visitors bureau. All of the following eateries are in Kissimmee:

Las Flores 7675 West Highway 192 (at Quality Inn); (305) 396-4000. American dining.

Aloha Restaurant & Lounge 7514 West Highway 192 (at Kon-Tiki Village Resort); (305) 396-2000. Polynesian/American cuisine. Reservations suggested.

Royal Palm Restaurant 7571 West Highway 192 (at Comfort Inn); (305) 396-7500. American cuisine in casual setting.

Tropic Isles 7300 West Highway 192 (at Holiday Inn Main Gate West); (305) 396-7300. Continental cuisine.

SLITHERING DOWN

When Houston trained in Cocoa, they would get an occasional snake in the area of the outfield fence, probably because a good part of the undeveloped acreage in Central Florida consists of marsh and swamp land. Snakes will pop up from time to time, usually in the most unexpected times and places.

Once in a gragefruit league game, Cesar Cedeno was playing center for the Astros. Now it must be pointed out that Cedeno had a legendary fear of snakes.

The batter hit a line drive to left center that went all the way to the wall. Cedeno broke quickly after the ball, as a good center fielder will, and tracked it down by the fence. As he reached down for the ball, he found it lying next to a big black snake that was sunning itself. The snake coiled itself around the ball.

Cedeno froze, then made a mad dash off the field, hopping a fence and retreating into the clubhouse. The batter got a ground-rule double. The fans were puzzled. The snake? Presumably it slithered quietly away to resume its siesta in a less disturbing locale.

Peking Gardens 4160 West Vine Street (on Highway 192); (305) 847-2266. Chinese food and steaks.

Cheffies Restaurant and Lounge 6075 Highway 192 (half mile east of Interstate 4); (305) 396-6100. Alligator tails, prime rib, seafood, ribs.

Sebastian's Seafood and Steak House 4980 West Spacecoast Parkway, Highway 192; (305) 396-0667. Features live Maine lobsters daily.

Rosario's 4838 Spacecoast Parkway; (305) 396-2204. Italian-American specialties. They also deliver within a four-mile radius.

Limey Jim's 6375 West Highway 192 (at the Hyatt); (305) 396-1234. A varied and elegant menu. This is a dressy place, and reservations are suggested.

The Mason Jar 5678 West Highway 192 (at Holiday Inn East); (305) 396-4488. Smorgasbord dining.

Olive Garden 5021 West Highway 192; (305) 396-1680. Italian cuisine. Reservations suggested.

Guiseppe's Italian Restaurant 3624 West Highway 192; (305) 847-9938. Italian food in a casual atmosphere.

Great Pastures Restaurant 4311 West Highway 192 (at Stagecoach Resort Inn); (305) 396-4213. Kosher meals.

Havana's Café 3628 West Highway 192; (305) 846-6771. A varied menu, with reservations suggested.

The Catfish Place 917 Bermuda Avenue (at the corner of Oak); (305) 847-9488. Seafood specialties.

Golden City Chinese Restaurant 1315 North Bermuda Avenue; (305) 933-4788. Chinese dining. Reservations suggested.

Steak & Ale 3405 West Highway 192; (305) 846-6603. Steak and beef specialties. Reservations suggested.

Kissimmee Steak Company 2047 East Highway 192 (at Green Parrot Plaza); (305) 847-8050. Beef house.

Shanghai Chinese Restaurant 1346 East Highway 192 (at Mill Creek Mall); (305) 933-2557. Chinese cuisine.

Blake's Restaurant 2145 East Highway 192 (at Holiday Inn Kissimmee); (305) 846-4646. American cuisine, casual atmosphere.

ATTRACTIONS The Kissimmee/St. Cloud area is literally in the middle of almost all Florida attractions: the Magic Kingdom of Disney World, Busch Gardens, Cypress Gardens, the Kennedy Space Center, and the beaches of the east and west coasts.

In the Kissimmee area itself, there is a variety of things to do:

Alligator Safari Zoo Florida wildlife is displayed along a mile-long trail. There are more than 1500 alligators. Hours are 9:00 A.M. to sunset daily. Located four miles west of downtown Kissimmee at 48580 West Highway 192; (305) 396-1012.

Gatorland Zoo This is a zoo, a commercial alligator farm, and a major research facility. Scenes from *Indiana Jones and the Temple of Doom* were filmed here. Located just north of town on Highway 441; (305) 855-5496.

Medieval Times Dinner Tournament Enjoy a unique dinner entertainment. Evening banquet and tournament are held in an eleventh-century-style castle. Tournament games and jousting are held while you put away a four-course meal. Located on West Highway 192; (305) 396-1518.

Pirate's Island Golf Two eighteen-hole courses are featured in this miniature golf park. Open from 9:00 A.M. to midnight daily on 4330 West Highway 192; (305) 396-4660.

Reptile World Serpentarium Can you handle close up views of cobras, pythons, and rattlesnakes? If so, this is the place for you. Open 9:00 A.M. to 5:30 P.M. Tuesday through Sunday. Located four miles east of St. Cloud on Highway 192; (305) 892-6905

Tupperware World Headquarters Now for something completely original. Get a guided tour of the company that's kept your food fresh for all these years. Open 9:00 A.M. to 4:00 P.M. Monday through Friday. Free admission. Located three miles north of Highway 192 on Highway 441; (305) 847-3111.

Water Mania This park has Florida's largest wave pool, also slides, flumes, volleyball, beaches, and picnic area. Located at 6073 West Highway 192; (305) 396-2626.

Xanadu Tour fifteen rooms of sculptured walls and computer-controlled gadgetry in this display of the Home of the Future. Located at the intersection of Highway 192 and State Road 535; (305) 396-1992.

All of the following shopping places are in Kissimmee:

Flea Market Factory Outlet 2301 West Vine Street, Spacecoast Parkway. No phone. One of the state's largest indoor flea markets.

Main Gate Outlet Mall Highway 192, one mile west of the Magic Kingdom entrance; (305) 396-4310. Many outlets, including Van Heusen and London Fog.

Nike Factory Outlet Highway 192; (305) 396-0500. Florida's only authentic Nike factory outlet. Selected closeouts and irregulars.

Osceola Square Mall 3831 West Vine Street; (305) 847-6941. Climate-controlled mall with WAL-MART, J. Byrons, many specialty shops.

Old Town   5770 Spacecoast Parkway (one and a quarter miles east of I-4 on Highway 192); (305) 396-4888. One of Florida's newest shopping, dining, and entertainment centers. More than seventy stores, a wood-carving museum, a hand-crafted antique carousel, and more. **Unique Army & Navy Stores**   3402 West Vine Street, Highway 192; (305) 846-1846. Tents, camouflage clothing, camping accessories, government surplus, and more. Rambo would love this place.

Fishing swimming, boating, sailing, golf, tennis, and camping are also part of the Kissimmee experience. Write or call the convention and visitors bureau for details.

> For more information, contact:
> **Kissimmee/St. Cloud Resort Area**
> **Convention and Visitors Bureau**
> **P.O. Box 2007**
> **Kissimmee 32742**
> **Out of state, toll free 1-800-327-9159**
> **In Florida, toll free 1-800-432-9199**

Lakeland

DETROIT TIGERS

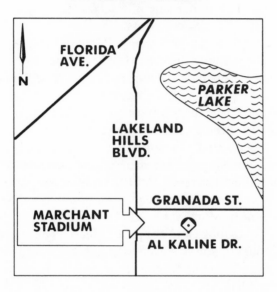

THE TEAM

The Lakeland-Detroit connection is one of the most enduring in all of baseball. Except for the war years of 1943 through 1945, when they trained in Evansville, Indiana, because of travel restrictions, the Tigers have held camp in Lakeland since 1934. Only the Cincinnati Reds, who have trained in Tampa since 1931, have a longer string in the same city.

TEAM HOTEL   Holiday Inn Central, 910 East Memorial Boulevard, Lakeland 33801; (813) 682-0101.

JOKER MARCHANT STADIUM From 1934 to 1966, the Tigers trained at Henry Field. Beginning in 1967, the team has called Joker Marchant its home park. You might be wondering about the unusual name. No, it wasn't named in honor of Cesar Romero's breathless portrayal of the Joker in the "Batman" TV series. It was named, instead, after the man instrumental in getting the stadium built.

The stadium is located one mile north of the old Henry Field site on Lakeland Hills Boulevard, in back of Parker Lake. The access road to the park is less cryptically dubbed: Al Kaline Drive. The all-concrete grandstand at Marchant Stadium was built by the city at a cost of $500,000 . . . a lot of money in 1967. In 1972, the Tigers played their first night game there under a new $160,000 set of lights. The stadium seats 4200, including 500 box seats.

Box seats are $5, general admission $4, with bleacher seats costing $2.50. Tickets go on sale at the box office beginning around February 20. The ticket office is open daily from 10:00 A.M. to 5:00 P.M., except for Sunday when the hours are from noon to 4:00 P.M. Tickets cannot be ordered by phone. They can only be purchased in person at the box office.

As you pull up to the park near game time, be prepared for a crunch of cars. The Tigers usually draw a full house. Attendants do their best to direct you into one of the nearby grassy fields to park your car, but sometimes the scene resembles the bumper cars at an amusement park. The best solution: get to the park early and leave late. And what's early? Game time at Marchant is 1:30 P.M., and 7:30 P.M. for occasional night games. Try to make it to the park at least a couple of hours early. If you pack a lunch, you can even enjoy an impromptu picnic. You'll also have time to enjoy batting practice. When the game ends, allow yourself about a half hour before leaving. By that time, the congestion will have eased up a bit.

Without fail, the P.A. announcer will implore everyone to "kindly squeeze a little closer together." This—along with such things as the country music played between innings, the grass fields and swaying palms surrounding the park, and the well-manicured diamond itself—gives a game in Lakeland a special quality.

Next to the stadium's twelve-acre property is Tigertown, the team's minor league training site since 1953. The bush leaguers trained there under spartan conditions until 1971, when the Tigers built a comfy, three-story, air-conditioned dormitory. It houses some 200 minor league players and officials.

Address and Phone Joker Marchant Stadium, Lakeland Hills Boulevard, Lakeland 33801; (813) 682-1401.

THE AREA

Lakeland has a sleepy, "Old South" quality about it . . . if you ignore the congested, claustrophobic nature of U.S. 92, a stretch of road with enough fast-food restaurants, blaring neon, and urban blight to last you about twenty-one vacations.

The city was established in 1884; the current population is 63,700. A dominant industry is oranges, with the Florida Citrus Commission headquartered in Lakeland. A Minute Maid plant is located in nearby Auburndale.

BEDDING DOWN The following establishments are all located within the city proper:

Best Western/Memorial Motor Lodge 508 East Memorial Boulevard (U.S. 92 and 98 at the junction of State Road 33); (813) 683-7471. 145 rooms, tennis, pool.

Days Inn 3223 U.S. 98 North (at the junction of I-4); (813) 688-6031. 239 rooms, restaurant.

Holiday Inn Central 910 East Memorial Boulevard; (813) 682-0101. 270 rooms, restaurant, tennis, two pools. Tiger team hotel.

Holiday Inn South 3405 South Florida Avenue; (813) 646-5731. 172 rooms, restaurant, entertainment, pool.

Howard Johnson's Motor Lodge 3425 U.S. 98 North; (813) 858-4481. 62 rooms, pool, restaurant.

The Huntley Inn U.S. 98 at I-4; (813) 688-8484. 155 rooms, pool.

Lake Parker Motel 1539 East Memorial Boulevard; (813) 683-7821. 43 rooms, pool, steam baths, near Marchant Stadium.

Quality Inn 3311 U.S. 98 North; (813) 688-7972. 120 rooms, pool, dining room, entertainment.

Red Carpet Inn 3410 U.S. 98 North; (813) 858-3851. 100 units, heated pool, restaurant.

Maryland Inn Motel 1433 Lakeland Hills Boulevard; (813) 683-6745. 34 rooms, 4 efficiencies.

MORSELS Except where noted, these restaurants are in Lakeland:

Foxfire U.S. 98 at junction of I-4; (813) 858-1481. Specialties include steak, seafood, prime rib. There's a nice salad bar, too.

Sea Wolf 4820 South Florida Avenue; (813) 646-2902. Seafood, steaks. Popular with the locals.

IT HAPPENED IN THE SPRING

Ernie Harwell, long-time and legendary voice of the Tigers, has a favorite spring training story:

"There are a lot of good spring training stories, but my favorite involves an infielder with the St. Louis Cardinals, Sam Narron. He was a rookie breaking in and Frankie Frisch was the player-manager of the Cardinals at the time. At spring training, Frank told all the rookies, 'When you come down here, I want you to pick out a guy and follow him; emulate what he does throughout spring training.'

"Sam was just sitting around, doing nothing, and when Frisch approached him, he said, 'I thought I told you to pick out a guy to emulate while you were here at spring training?' Narron replied, 'I did. I picked you.' "

Lakeland, with the lake nearby, can be a windy place.

"I remember one game between Boston and Detroit. Jim Rice got a ball in the air, and my partner, Jon Miller's, description went like this: 'There's a pop fly near second base. It's still going out over second base, going out toward right center field, and now it's going over the fence, for a home run.' Jon's call was accurate.
—**Ken Coleman**

And things can get rough.

"One of the strangest things I've ever seen in a spring training camp was in 1981, the time Jim Rice and then-Boston PR Director Bill Crowley tangled outside the batting cage at Lakeland. Rice had earlier that day parked his '57 Chevy in Crowley's space near the Sox clubhouse in Winter Haven.

"Crowley, despite being near retirement age, confronted Rice, one of the strongest men in baseball, about the incident. In the ensuing shouting and shoving match, Rice pulled the skin off the top of Crowley's hand.

"All this happened on Friday the 13th."
—**Dan Valenti**

Strollo's 1295 East Main Street; (813) 683-4866. Italian-American menu. Specialties include lasagna, ravioli, manicotti.

Talk of the Town Steakhouse 735 East Main Street; (813) 686-1434. Specialties include steak, prime rib, seafood.

Frog's Oyster House 3120 South Florida Avenue; (813) 686-8345. Fresh seafood, oysters, charbroiled steaks.

Black Forest Buffet Restaurant U.S. 27, Lake Wales; (813) 638-3036. It's about a thirty-six mile drive from Lakeland, but the food is worth the drive. Buffets each evening. Friday specialty is crab legs; Saturday it's German buffet.

The Mark One 304 East Lemon Street; (813) 687-6275. Dinner theater—enjoy a play and a meal. Munchie menu in lounge.

Morrison's 1108 East Memorial Boulevard; (813) 688-6482. Cafeteria-style dining. Morrison's is probably the best restaurant buy in Florida. Delicious food, great prices.

Sampan Restaurant 1521 U.S. 98 South (at Grove Plaza); (813) 688-9977. Oriental and American cuisine. Children's menu available.

You'll also find the usual assortment of fast-food restaurants in Lakeland (there are so many of them, they seem to find you). For other dining options, try nearby Winter Haven.

ATTRACTIONS Compared to other parts of Florida, Lakeland is not a real "doing" kind of place, once you get past the Tigers. But its Central Florida location makes it an excellent base from which to do serious touring elsewhere. Still, there are a few attractions you should check out:

Florida Southern College McDonald Street and Ingraham Avenue. Park in the main lot on Johnson Avenue, midway between McDonald Street and Lake Hollingsworth. The college has the world's largest collection of buildings designed by Frank Lloyd Wright. Wright worked on what he called "organic" buildings here, beginning in 1938 with the Annie Pfeiffer Chapel. Tours are self-guided, with maps available in the administration building. Call the chamber of commerce for phone number and other information at (813) 688-8551.

Bok Tower Gardens In Mt. Lake Sanctuary, about three miles north of Lake Wales off U.S. Highway 27-A (about forty miles from Lakeland). The gardens offer a magnificent place to escape into restful quiet. The 205-foot stone tower houses a fifty-three-bell carillon. Concerts daily at 3:00 P.M. The gardens are open daily beginning at 8:00 A.M. Gates close at 5:30 P.M.

Citrus World U.S. Highway 27 just north of Lake Wales. If you go to Bok Tower Gardens, you're about four miles from Citrus World. Open Monday through Friday, 9:00 A.M. to 4:30 P.M. Film tour follows the production of orange juice, from grove to supermarket. Gift shop and a free glass of juice. Another juice-related attraction is the **Minute Maid** plant in Auburndale, eleven miles east of Lakeland on U.S. 92. Tours are given daily.

In Lakeland, you'll find an assortment of outdoor activities, from boating and fishing on the many lakes to golf and tennis. Contact the chamber of commerce.

> For more information, contact:
> **Lakeland Chamber of Commerce**
> **35 Lake Morton Drive**
> **P.O. Box 3538**
> **Lakeland 33802**
> **(813) 688-8551**

Orlando

MINNESOTA TWINS

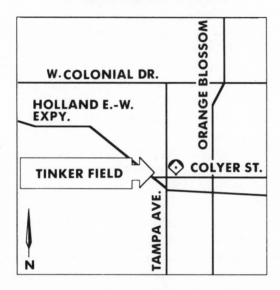

THE TEAM

Counting the years when the franchise was the Washington Senators (they became the Minnesota Twins in 1961), the Twins have been in Orlando since 1936. The only exception came in the war years of 1943 and '44, when the club trained in College Park, Maryland.

TEAM HOTEL Court of Flags, 5715 Major Boulevard, Orlando 32819; (305) 351-3340.

TINKER FIELD   Tinker is a little gumdrop of a park set close to downtown Orlando. The park is named after Joe Tinker of Tinker-to-Evans-to-Chance fame (by the way, the third baseman of that infield was Harry Steinfeldt). Tinker played a major part in bringing major league baseball to Orlando in the 1930s.

The current stadium was built in 1963, with a capacity of about 5500, though more can be squeezed in if necessary. Look for the three-ton memorial to the former owner of the Senators, Clark Griffith. The tribute to the Washington origins of the Twins' bloodline continues in the stands itself: about 500 wooden seats from Washington's old Griffith Stadium are located in the upper part of the covered grandstand.

Down the right field line and across the right field wall, the Citrus Bowl towers over Tinker Field. When you focus your eyes there, you feel as if you're in a tugboat anchored next to an aircraft carrier.

The field is kept immaculately clean and manicured; the grass seems greener than green, almost the kind of green you'd see in a film shot in Technicolor. In the morning and early afternoon, the sun drenches the stadium (no doubt, it was designed that way); that, combined with the chummy dimensions of the park, leaves you in an ideal frame of mind to enjoy a springtime baseball game.

Pitchers and catchers on the forty-man roster report sometime around February 20 or 21. The rest of the roster arrives at the end of the month. Minor leaguers train in Melbourne, on the east coast and to the south, between Cocoa and Vero Beach.

As with most Florida stadiums, Tinker Field is not an easy place to get in and out of on the day of a game. Tickets to grapefruit league games can be obtained only at the Tinker box office or by mail. The box office is open 9:30 A.M. to 5:00 P.M. Monday through Friday and 10:00 A.M. to 2:00 P.M. on Saturday. Box seats are $6 and reserved grandstand $5. General admission, sold only on the day of the game, is $3. Game time is 1:30 P.M.

To order tickets by mail, send check or money order to the Minnesota Twins, P.O. Box 5645, Orlando 32855. Include $1 for postage.

Address and Phone   Tinker Field, 287 Tampa Avenue S., Orlando 32805; (305) 351-3340.

THE AREA

When you mention Orlando to a baseball fan, he will say, "Twins." But anyone else will respond with "Walt Disney World." Disney is the

Magic Kingdom and power that, more than any other single factor, led to the development boom (some would call it a plague) that is under way in (again, some would say "has infected") Central Florida. Disney World is simply the most popular tourist attraction on earth.

Comedian Steve Wright once asked what would happen if you were driving at the speed of light and you turned your headlights on. The answer is you would find yourself in Orlando. Led on by Disney, land prices have shot up astronomically, and over $14 billion in new construction is set to be completed by 1990. The tourist attractions generate $2 billion a year, helping Orlando retail stores to jingle up about $4.6 billion a year.

Is this kingdom really magic, as backers contend? Or is it more like the Sorcerer's Apprentice finally having his revenge, with a nightmare about to get out of hand? It's hard to say. Central Florida's population has rocketed, and land that was going for $200 an acre a few years ago now fetches $200,000 an acre. Good or bad? It depends on your own priorities. In fact, only the years will judge the outcome. But for now there's no arguing: the (Mickey) Mouse that roared has created an undeniable impact, and things will never be the same.

BEDDING DOWN Orlando, at 60,000 rooms, ranks second only to New York City in the country for the town with the most hotel space. Here's a partial listing (all properties are in Orlando, except where noted):

The Comfort Inn of Orlando 8421 South Orange Blossom Trail; (305) 855-6060 or toll free 1-800-327-9742.

Crowne Plaza/Orlando 7527 Currency Drive; (305) 859-1500.

Days Inn of America 2500 West 23rd Street; (305) 841-3731 or toll free 1-800-325-2525.

Econo-Lodge International 8738 International Drive; (305) 345-8195.

Economy Motels of America/International Drive 8222 Jamaican Court; (305) 345-1172.

Embassy Suites Plaza International 8250 Jamaican Court; (305) 345-8250 or toll free 1-800-327-9797.

Gateway Inn 7050 Kirkman Road; (305) 351-2000 or toll free 1-800-327-3808.

The Harley Hotel of Orlando 151 East Washington Street; (305) 841-3220 or toll free 1-800-321-2323.

Hilton Inn Florida Center 7400 International Drive; (305) 351-4600 or toll free 1-800-327-1363.

Hilton at Walt Disney World Village 1751 Hotel Plaza Boulevard, Lake Buena Vista; (305) 827-4000 or toll free 1-800-432-5141.

Holiday Inn/Disney World Area 6515 International Drive; (305) 351-3500 or toll free 1-800-HOLIDAY.

Holiday Inn/Lee Road 626 Lee Road; (305) 645-5600 or toll free 1-800-HOLIDAY.

Howard Johnson's Downtown 304 West Colonial Drive; (305) 843-8700 or toll free 1-800-654-2000.

Hyatt Regency/Grand Express One Grand Cypress Boulevard; (305) 239-1234 or toll free 1-800-228-9000.

Knights Inn 5909 American Way; (305) 351-6500.

Las Palmas Inn 6233 International Drive; (305) 351-3900.

Omni International Hotel/Orlando Centroplex 400 West Livingston Street; (305) 843-6664.

Orlando Airport Marriott 7499 Augusta National Drive; (305) 851-9000 or toll free 1-800-228-9290.

Orlando Marriott 8001 International Drive; (305) 351-2420 or toll free 1-800-228-9290.

Park Suite Hotel 8978 International Drive; (305) 352-1400.

Quality Inn Plaza 9000 International Drive; (305) 345-8585.

Radisson Plaza Hotel Orlando 60 South Ivanhoe Boulevard; (305) 425-4455.

Ramada Inn Central 4919 West Colonial Drive; (305) 288-8180 or toll free 1-800-327-6908.

Sheraton/Colonial Plaza Motor Inn 2801 East Colonial Drive; (305) 894-2741 or toll free 1-800-325-3535.

Sheraton Inn/Winter Park 736 Lee Road; (305) 647-1112 or toll free 1-800-325-3535.

Sheraton Twin Towers 5780 Major Boulevard; (305) 351-1000 or toll free 1-800-327-2110.

Sonesta Village Hotel 10000 Turkey Lake Road; (305) 352-8051 or toll free 1-800-343-7170.

Super 8 Motel 5859 American Way; (305) 345-8880.

Thriftway Inns of America 5900 American Way; (305) 352-8383 or toll free 1-800-321-2467.

TraveLodge Gardens 7101 South Orange Blossom Trail; (305) 851-4300 or toll free 1-800-255-3050.

Village Hotel Plaza Association 1905 Hotel Plaza Boulevard, Lake Buena Vista; (305) 828-2828.

Viscount Hotel 2000 Hotel Plaza Boulevard, Lake Buena Vista; (305) 828-2424.

Wyndham Hotel at Sea World 6677 Sea Harbor Drive; (305) 351-6695.

MORSELS There are simply too many restaurants in the Orlando area to list them all. We present a sampling here. Write the chamber of commerce for a more complete listing if you need it. Unless otherwise noted, these places are in Orlando.

But before we begin the listing, we should give special notice to Rosie O'Grady's Goodtime Emporium. This collection of bars, restaurants, and shops is located in the old Orlando Hotel across from the Church Street Station. If you can't find a good time here, something's amiss. The names of some of the restaurants will give you a good idea of what kind of place this is. Included are Apple Annie's Courtyard Restaurant, the Cheyenne Saloon and Opera House, Lili Marlene's Aviators' Pub and Restaurant, and Phineas Phogg's Balloon Works, "purveyors of balloons, burgers, and boogie." Phogg's even offers champagne balloon flights. If you have a few extra grand to blow, say between $6000 and $12,000, you can even walk away with your own hot-air balloon. Think of the air fare you'll save on the way home.

The Bavarian Inn of Orlando 61 East Church Street; (305) 425-4060.
Casa Gallardo 8250 International Drive; (305) 352-9191.
Chi-Chi's Sombrero Restaurants 7447 Orange Blossom Trail; (305) 896-4830.
Christini's Ristorante Italiano 7600 Phillips Boulevard; (305) 345-8770.
Gary's Duck Inn 3974 South Orange Blossom Trail; (305) 843-0270.
Bill Knapp's Restaurant 8348 International Drive; (305) 345-0861.
La Normandie Restaurant 2021 East Colonial Drive; (305) 896-9976.
Lee's Lakeside 431 East Central Boulevard; (305) 841-1565.
O'Scarlett's Restaurant 6308 International Drive; (305) 345-0727.
The Olive Garden 3675 East Colonial Drive; (305) 859-3044.
Park Plaza Gardens Restaurant 319 Park Avenue S., Winter Park; (305) 645-2475.
Piccadilly Restaurant & Pub 7100 South Orange Blossom Trail; (305) 855-0050.
Quincy's Family Steak House 5831 South Orange Blossom Trail; (305) 859-4721.
Ran-Getsu of Tokyo 8400 International Drive; (305) 345-0044.
Ronnie's Restaurant Colonial Shopping Plaza; (305) 894-4951.

". . . TO SEE HOW I'D LOOK"

To come into camp in 1962 as a rookie was exciting. I always wanted to get the chance to come to a spring training camp with big-league ball players to see how I'd look. I knew in my mind it would take a miracle for me to make the Minnesota Twins ball club.

"I never thought of the pressure. That's the way I played the game. I didn't put pressure on myself. I knew my hitting was there; I could hit anybody. But I knew I had to work very hard on my fielding.

"Nobody likes to be sent down. Any time they send you down, you should make up your mind to do better. If you've just come off a year in Double A and they send you down, make up your mind to kill Triple A. If you go down, you should have the attitude 'Hey, if I go to Double A, I'm going to kill it. If I go to Triple A, I'm going to kill it. Because I belong in the big leagues.' Show them that you belong in the big leagues. But if you get sent down and you feel sorry for yourself and have a bad year, you're gonna hurt yourself.

"That was my attitude when I was sent down in '62 and '63. I went to Triple A and had a great year. The next year ('64), the Twins gave me the opportunity to play every day in right field, and I played there for eight straight years."
—**Tony Oliva**

Samurai Japanese Steak House   3911 East Colonial Drive; (305) 896-9696.

Sukiyaki House   2809 Corrine Drive; (305) 894-5081.

Western Sizzlin' Steak House   351 North Orlando Avenue, Winter Park; (305) 628-1121.

ATTRACTIONS   What need we say but one word? "Disney."

Probably the only way one can really say what Walt Disney World is like is by analogy. The Magic Kingdom is to the Orlando area like Mao was to China during the Cultural Revolution. Everywhere, the image. Organized, orchestrated, Orwellian, even.

The sheer size of Disney World overwhelms. You are swallowed. When you exit from I-4, you may think you're there . . . keep driving. After you go a way, you'll pull into a flatland 12,000-space parking lot. You then board a tram for a journey to the main gate, where you can buy tickets. From there, it's a monorail or boat ride to the famous castle. After all this, you're just about to begin your day (or days) at the park.

It would be pointless here to try to give you the full flavor of Disney World. Entire books have been written about this extravaganza, and still there's more to say. We can say that the Magic Kingdom is divided into theme parks. The best way to see as much as possible is to see them in this order: Adventureland (tropical locales), Frontierland (pioneering life), Liberty Square (Hall of Presidents, the Haunted Mansion), Fantasyland (childhood favorites), and Tomorrowland (Mission to Mars and Space Mountain).

Crowds at this tourist wonder are immense . . . Disney World out-draws most countries as a vacation spot. So be prepared to wait. The Disney people have perfected waiting to a science: a forty-minute line into a ride will look deceptively small because of the way they snake people around in a tiny space.

The best piece of advice we can give on dealing with the huddled masses at Disney World: "do the opposite." By that we mean, reverse your normal patterns. Don't eat lunch at lunchtime, or dinner at dinner-time, because that's when everyone else will do it. Try to arrive the very minute the gates open (9:00 A.M.). If you wait until mid to late morning, you'll be stuck. The best time to get into an attraction without a long wait is at the very end of the day.

To see eveything in Disney World, you'll need a few days. Disney offers a five-day World Passport that will cover everything in the Magic Kingdom and EPCOT Center.

EPCOT is different from the Magic Kingdom. There are no thrill rides or Mickey Mouse, but a lot of educational exhibits . . . and lasers, and holograms, and Spaceship Earth, and trips through time, and 3D movies so lifelike you'll get confused as to what is real and what is film, and so on.

There's so much going on, so much entertainment, so many shows at Disney World that the schedule changes daily. Consult the Disney PR staff, brochures, and posted schedules when you arrive at the park.

To get to the Magic Kingdom, take Highway 536 via Interstate 4. Hours are 9:00 A.M. to 10:00 P.M. To get to EPCOT Center, take Highway 192 via Interstate 4. EPCOT hours are 9:00 A.M. to 9:00 P.M. For information on both, call (305) 824-4321.

Is there life after Disney in the Orlando area? Yes. Here are a few of the "other" attractions:

Sea World   7007 Sea World Drive (I-4 and the Beeline Expressway); (305) 351-3600. This marine park features killer whale, seal, dolphin, and walrus shows.

Wet 'n Wild   6200 Orlando Drive; (305) 351-1800. This twenty-five-acre water park has rides, slides, and waves.

Elvis Presley Museum   5931 American Way (near International Drive); (305) 345-8860. Houses 300 Elvis items, including guitars, cars, and wardrobe.

Fun 'n Wheels   6739 Sand Lake Road; (305) 351-5651. Amusement park featuring bumper cars, go-carts, mini-golf, and kiddie rides.

Mystery Fun House   At the intersection of I-4 and Highway 435 (Kirkman Road). Magic floors, laughing doors, mirror maze, and more.

And on and on it goes, from golfing and tennis to fishing and boating. Also, don't forget shopping. There's lots of it in the Orlando area. Here are a few selected malls:

Altamonte Mall   I-4 to State Road 436 to Altamonte Springs exit, east; (305) 830-4400.

Colonial Plaza Mall   I-4 east to Colonial Drive exit (Highway 50), east about two miles to Bumby Avenue; (305) 894-3601.

Orlando Fashion Square   I-4 east to Colonial Drive exit (Highway 50), due east about four miles. (305) 855-1131.

For more information, contact:
Greater Orlando Chamber of Commerce
75 East Ivanhoe Boulevard
P.O. Box 1234
Orlando 32802
(305) 425-1234

Winter Haven

BOSTON RED SOX

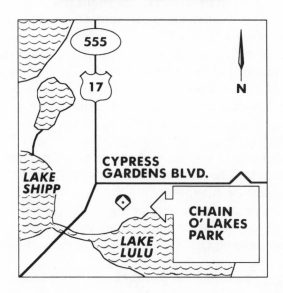

THE TEAM

Boston gave up the ghost in Scottsdale, Arizona, following the 1965 season; in 1966, the club moved to the quiet town of Winter Haven. At that time, there were a couple of hotels and restaurants in town, and not much else. The team hotel was the delapidated Haven.

But the influx of New Englanders who make their annual visit has meant a lot to the local economy over the years. One example is the Haven, which has been reborn into a current life of luxury condos. Add the fact that Winter Haven has ridden rather comfortably on the tails of the development of Central Florida in general, and what you get is a still small but growing town with nice places at which to stay, eat, and visit.

TEAM HOTEL Holiday Inn, 1150 Third Street S.W. (on U.S. 17), Winter Haven 33880; (813) 294-4451.

CHAIN O' LAKES PARK The reason for the park's name is that it's situated literally on a chain of lakes that connect to each other by canals. In fact, there are about one hundred lakes in the city. One general reminder about the lakes in Florida: most of them have alligators, so be alert, especially when you are walking near undeveloped shoreline.

Boston's forty-man roster begins arriving in late February, with batterymen arriving about the 21st. The rest of the squad reports on March 1. The minor leaguers arrive sometime around the middle of March, and they train at the four and a half playing fields below Chain O' Lakes.

Before the minor leaguers arrive, the Sox split their squads, half training at the stadium, and the other half occupying the first of the lower diamonds. Perhaps the best way to catch an autograph or a chat or an up-close view of a Red Sox player is to hang around just outside that first lower diamond around 10:00 A.M., when workouts begin. The players walk by there and enter through a gate in the right field fence. Just remember that if you see a player at that time, he's on his way to "the office," that is, reporting for work, so don't be annoying or bothersome. Just be friendly.

After the minor leaguers arrive, the big club's action is strictly limited to the stadium. But the baseball fan has one compelling reason to spend some time on the lower fields. That reason's name is Theodore Samuel Williams.

Ted usually arrives from the Florida Keys by mid-March, and spends most of his time instructing minor leaguers on the fine points of hitting. With Ted's booming presence and your closeness to the field, you'll be able to hear every word, and it's hard to describe what a thrill this can be.

Your time spent at Chain O' Lakes Park will be as pleasant. The stadium underwent some changes in 1987, including additional seating, bringing capacity to about 4600 (though they once squeezed 6196 in for the Yankees on March 22, 1979), and a $100,000 electronic scoreboard. Other improvements included a 750-foot clubhouse expansion and the installation of 3000 chair-back grandstand seats. Additional changes are on tap, making this comfortable ballpark even better.

From the fan's perspective, watching major league baseball doesn't get any better than it is at Chain O' Lakes. All of the seats offer great views, you are close to the action, the park is immaculately clean and well groomed . . . come to think of it, what you'll get is almost a Florida equivalent of Fenway Park. The nearby orange groves will add a pleasant orange fragrance to the air. Combine all this with a sun-washed Florida day, and you'll find baseball nirvana.

Ticket prices are $4 for grandstand and $5 for box seats, and tickets can be purchased in advance, beginning in late February, or on the day of the game. We will repeat a tip we've mentioned several times in this book: arrive early and stay late. You'll not only enjoy an unhurried time at the park, but you'll also avoid the crowds.

Address and Phone Chain O' Lakes Park, Cypress Gardens Boulevard, Winter Haven 33880; (813) 293-3900.

THE AREA

Winter Haven is a small town in a beautiful setting of spring-fed lakes, rolling countryside, and orange groves. The dominant industries are citrus and tourism.

As the other towns of Central Florida, Winter Haven's location in the geographical center of the Florida peninsula makes it ideal as a base of operation for touring the rest of the state or visiting a number of baseball camps. It's convenient to just about all of the state.

BEDDING DOWN Accommodations are varied. You won't get the selection that you'll find in a town like Tampa or Orlando, but you won't pay as much for your room, either. All of the following are in Winter Haven:

Landmark Motor Lodge 1965 U.S. Highway 17 North (at junction of State Road 544); (813) 294-4231 or toll free 1-800-528-1234. Rooms, efficiencies, dining room, lounge, sauna bath, near two eighteen-hole golf courses.

Comfort Inn 200 Cypress Gardens Boulevard; (813) 299-1151. 104 rooms, full-service restaurant, tennis, and Olympic pool.

Howard Johnson's Motor Lodge 1300 U.S. Highway 17 South; (813) 294-7321 or toll free 1-800-654-2000. Restaurant, pub, miniature golf course, heated pool.

Lake Roy Motor Lodge 1823 Cypress Gardens Boulevard; (813) 324-6320. Private white sand beach, boat ramp on lake, near three golf courses, all rooms with lake views.

Tropic Motel 401 Sixth Street N.W. (Highway 17); (813) 294-4191. Downtown location. Rooms or efficiencies, near shopping, restaurants.

TENNIS, ANYONE?

In 1980, Carl Yastrzemski was still playing. Ted Williams was in camp as an instructor. The two men had always been compared to each other, since Yaz replaced Williams in left field in 1961. Both men were avid tennis players. Ted was about sixty years old, but very agile on his feet, and he had these enormous arms, very long, which helped him become such a great hitter. And Yaz, nearing the end of his career, was still a great athlete.

"In camp that year, the two agreed to a match. It was like a great confrontation about to take place. You could have billed it like a World Wrestling Federation main event. It had a larger-than-life quality to it. So they met at the Ramada Inn a couple of hours after practice. Word of the match got around after the reporters heard of it, and about one hundred people showed up to watch.

"It wasn't a recreational match, and they didn't play it like fun. Yaz took pride in his athletic ability, and he went after the old man. But to his shock and horror, he saw Williams like a giant condor at the net. Every time Yaz would hit a really hard serve to Ted's forehand or backhand, Ted would charge the net, and with those enormous arms, he could reach anything, and he would just tap the ball back. He moved Yaz from one side of the court to the other. Yaz was constantly making spectacular shots just to get the ball back.

"Yaz was so shocked he lost the first match 6–2. Ted got a standing ovation. As the match continued, the difference in age between the two men began to show. They played three sets. Yaz started to lob, and Ted just couldn't get back. Toward the third set, Yaz wore him down. But by that time, everyone was roaring in laughter. It was the highlight of the spring to watch this titanic struggle between two legends."
—**Larry Whiteside,** *Boston Globe* **sportswriter**

Lake Ida Beach Resort and Motel   2524 North U.S. Highway 17; (813) 293-0942 or toll free 1-800-233-7152. Rooms, efficiencies, or cottages. Private dock and pier.

Camellia Motel   820 Sixth Street N.W. (Highway 17); (813) 293-5844 or 293-5845. Rooms or apartments, heated pool.

Cypress Motel & Trailer Park   5651 Cypress Gardens Boulevard; (813) 324-5867 or toll free 1-800-322-8029. Rooms and efficiencies, pool, gift shop.

Garden Lodge Motel   2000 Cypress Gardens Boulevard; (813) 324-6334. Rooms, efficiencies, or apartments; pool; satellite TV; near fishing and golfing.

Holiday Inn of Winter Haven   1150 Third Street S.W. (on Highway 17); (813) 294-4451. Team hotel for the Red Sox. Paddy O'Shea's Restaurant and Lounge, pool.

Banyon Beach Motel   1630 Sixth Street (U.S. Highway 17 Northwest); (813) 293-3658 or (813) 293-3788. Rooms amid tropical setting, heated pool, private beach.

The Ranch House Motor Inn   1911 Cypress Garden Boulevard; (813) 324-5994. Fully equipped efficiencies and apartments, restaurant, miniature golf course.

Quality Inn Town House Motor Lodge   975 Cypress Gardens Boulevard; (813) 294-4104.

Red Carpet Inn   2000 Cypress Gardens Boulevard; (813) 324-6334.

Sunshine Motel   3560 U.S. Highway 17 North; (813) 299-3771.

Rose Motel   815 Sixth Street N.W.; (813) 294-4201.

MORSELS   Winter Haven boasts a number of fine restaurants. All the following are in town:

Lombardo's Italian Cuisine   636 West Central Avenue; (813) 294-3426. Delicious Italian specialties. Reservations suggested.

Mario's Restaurant   3601 Cypress Gardens Boulevard; (813) 324-6355. Another fine Italian restaurant.

Christy's Sundown Restaurant   U.S. Highway 17 South (adjacent to the Holiday Inn); (813) 294-6073 or 293-0069. One of the finest restaurants in all of Florida, serving prime rib, Maine lobsters, charbroiled steaks, fresh seafood, and stone crab. Recommended by AAA.

Charlie's Park Café   505 Avenue A N.W.; (813) 299-2325. Live Maine lobster, prime ribs of beef, fresh New England and Florida seafood, early-bird specials, piano bar.

Andy's Drive-In Restaurant 703 Third Street S.W.; (813) 293-0019. Good food, great prices.

Sonny's Real Pit Bar-B-Q Corner of Recker Highway at Avenue G N.W.; (813) 293-4744. Ribs that will give you a taste of the South. Nice salad bar, too.

Golden Gate Chinese Restaurant 1000 Cypress Gardens Boulevard; (813) 299-4998. Cantonese and Mandarin cuisine, takeout orders.

Harriston's Restaurant 3751 Cypress Gardens Boulevard; (813) 324-0301. Steaks, seafood, poultry, and lamb creatively prepared.

Red Lobster 401 Third Street S.W. (on U.S. 17); (813) 294-8844. Seafood and steaks, plus daily specials.

Little Caesar's WAL-MART Shopping Plaza, Cypress Gardens Boulevard; (813) 293-7000. Pizzas, sandwiches, salads. Carryout only.

Sea Flame 2601 Havendale Boulevard; (813) 965-2871. Prime rib, pasta, seafood, and specials.

Hungry Howdie's Pizzas & Subs North Gate Square, 1144 Sixth Street N.W.; (813) 293-4633. Pizzas, subs, and salads for dining in or taking out.

Morrison's Cafeteria 140 Winter Haven Mall; (813) 293-1003. For the price and the great food quality, maybe the best restaurant buy in town. The food's always delicious, and the lines move quickly.

Sea Gallery 200 Cypress Gardens Boulevard; (813) 299-2535. Next to Chain O' Lakes Park. Seafood, chicken, steak, and a great salad bar.

Tony's Italian Restaurant 448 Cypress Gardens Boulevard; (813) 294-6875. Moderately priced, family-style restaurant very popular with members of the Red Sox. Steaks, seafood, chicken, house specials.

Sally's Shrimp Boat 1006 Lake Howard Drive S.W.; (813) 293-5567. Beef, crab legs, and boat tours.

Nostalgia U.S. Highway 17 North; (813) 299-4810. Seafood, steaks, prime rib, and French cuisine. Reservations requested.

Antiquarian 371 Third Street N.W.; (813) 294-5464. Chicken, filet mignon, seafood, veal.

J.W.'s Old Fashioned Eatery 1915 Cypress Gardens Boulevard; (813) 324-3222. Ribs, steak, seafood.

ATTRACTIONS After the Sox, the first place to go is Cypress Gardens.

Cypress Gardens Located just east of Winter Haven on Cypress Gardens Boulevard; (813) 324-2111. The magnificent gardens draw visitors from all over the world. The fun includes ski shows, boat rides, a winding walkway through some of the most beautiful plants in the world, and the naturally landscaped Living Forest, with live animals.

Black Hills Passion Play Located 1½ miles south of Lake Wales on U.S. 27A; (813) 676-1495. Runs through the Lenten season in an amphitheater. The suffering and resurrection of Christ are portrayed in a lavish production.

Water Ski Museum/Hall of Fame Located on State Road 550 at Carl Floyd Road three miles off U.S. 27, five miles east of Winter Haven. Exhibits feature the history of water skiing and memorabilia. Free.

Also, Winter Haven offers great opportunities for fishing, boating, golf, tennis. The town's public golf course is Willowbrook Golf Club, 4200 Highway 544 North; (813) 294-5508. Theater groups at Polk Community College and the Winter Haven Community Theater offer fine stage productions. The area also offers indoor roller skating and horseback riding.

For more information, contact:
The Winter Haven Chamber of Commerce
101 Sixth Street N.W.
P.O. Box 1420
Winter Haven 33882
(813) 293-2138

Ft. Lauderdale
NEW YORK YANKEES

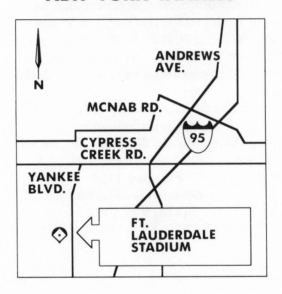

THE TEAM

The Ft. Lauderdale area, like Miami and West Palm Beach, is an area that people generally know something about. They have a good idea of what to expect there. It's a city of beaches, racetracks, night life, and the Yankees.

The Yanks have been training in Ft. Lauderdale since 1962, on the crest of the Mantle-Maris wave that was soon to crash on the shore of mediocrity in the mid-sixties.

TEAM HOTEL Ft. Lauderdale Marriott Cypress Creek, 6650 North Andrews Avenue, Ft. Lauderdale 33309; (305) 771-0440.

FT. LAUDERDALE STADIUM   This park is one of the best in Florida, a wonderful place from which to watch a ball game. The Yanks, of course, are the major tenant of the stadium. They'll draw over 100,000 each spring. It's one of the bigger spring parks, with a capacity of about 7500 and on-site parking for 3500 cars. It's 335 feet down the left field foul line, 401 to center, and 325 to right.

It has a first-class lighting system, sufficient for network television broadcast. There are three concession stands in the park, as well as handicapped-accessible rest rooms.

The Yanks usually report earlier than most teams: batterymen about February 20, the full squad about February 25. Space limitations mean that only the Yankees and their Triple A farm hands can train at the Ft. Lauderdale facility. The rest of the minor leaguers train in nearby Hollywood.

The stadium is owned by the city. The Yankees current lease began in 1982 and runs through 1988. There's an option for the years 1989 through 1992. The Yanks turn over to the city 15 percent of the gross receipts from ticket sales. It will be interesting to see what happens after 1988. As we've mentioned elsewhere in this book, competition among Florida cities for a major league team is intensifying. Don't be surprised to see some area make a major pitch for the Yankees, with one of the points being the fact that the Yanks can't fit their minor league system under the Ft. Lauderdale roof.

When the Yankees head north, the stadium is home to the Ft. Lauderdale Yankees of the A-level Florida State League. The city also rents the facility for the Mickey Mantle–Whitey Ford Fantasy Baseball Camp, concerts, and professional wrestling matches.

Tickets to exhibition games at Ft. Lauderdale Stadium cost $8.50 for boxes, $7 for reserved, and $4 for general admission. There's a $2 fee for parking. The stadium is located three blocks west of Interstate 95 just north of Commercial Boulevard.

Address and Phone   Ft. Lauderdale Stadium, 5301 Northwest 12th Avenue, Ft. Lauderdale 33309; (305) 776-1921.

THE AREA

Some 3000 hours of sunshine a year, 50 golf courses, 500 tennis courts, deep-sea fishing, torrid night life, the mysterious Everglades, and 6½ miles of beach front — all this in the Ft. Lauderdale area. If that's not the formula for excitement, nothing is. Unless you are a baseball junkie, you just might find yourself turning an erstwhile trip to spring training into an immersion in this "Venice of America," so named for the series of canals that link city neighborhoods.

BEDDING DOWN   As with any major town (population 1 million) —especially a resort town of Ft. Lauderdale's reputation—you'll find a huge selection of accommodations, to fit any budget and level of comfort. For a complete list, contact the chamber of commerce. Here's a sampling, all of them in the city, unless otherwise noted:

Alhambra Beach   3021 Alhambra Street; (305) 462-1021. 10 units.

Bahia Cabana   3001 Harbor Drive; (305) 524-1555 or toll free 1-800-BEACHES. 115 rooms.

Bonaventure Hotel   250 Racquet Club Road; (305) 389-3300 or toll free 1-800-327-8090. 504 rooms.

Breakers of Ft. Lauderdale   909 Breakers Avenue; (305) 566-8800. 181 rooms.

Embassy Suites Ft. Lauderdale North   555 Northwest 62nd Street; (305) 772-5400 or toll free 1-800-EMBASSY. 258 rooms.

Embassy Suites Ft. Lauderdale South   1100 Southeast 17th Street Causeway; (305) 527-2700 or toll free 1-800-EMBASSY. 363 rooms.

Ft. Lauderdale Motel   501 Southeast 17th Street; (305) 525-5194. 90 units.

Golden Sands   519 North Birch Road; (305) 563-6265. 22 units.

Holiday Inn Ft. Lauderdale Beach   999 North Atlantic Boulevard; (305) 563-5961 or toll free 1-800-HOLIDAY. 242 rooms.

Holiday Inn Oceanside   3000 East Las Olas Boulevard; (305) 463-8421 or toll free 1-800-HOLIDAY. 224 rooms.

Hollywood Beach Hilton   4000 South Ocean Drive, Hollywood; (305) 458-1900. 312 rooms.

Howard Johnson's Ocean Edge   700 North Atlantic Boulevard; (305) 563-2451 or toll free 1-800-327-8578. 144 rooms.

Ireland's Inn   2220 North Atlantic Boulevard; (305) 565-6661 or toll free 1-800-327-4460. 81 rooms.

Lauderdale Beach Hotel   101 South Atlantic Avenue; (305) 764-0088 or toll free 1-800-327-7600.

Lauderdale Biltmore   435 North Atlantic Beach; (305) 462-0444. 81 units.

Marina Inn & Yacht Harbor   2150 Southeast 17th Street; (305) 525-3484 or toll free 1-800-327-1390. 176 rooms.

Marriott Cypress Creek   I-95 at Cypress Creek Road; (305) 771-0440. 322 rooms.

Marriott's Harbor Beach Resort   3030 Holiday Drive; (305) 525-4000 or toll free 1-800-228-9290. 645 rooms.
Ocean Manor Resort Hotel   4040 Galt Ocean Drive; (305) 566-7500 or toll free 1-800-327-8874. 168 rooms.
Princess Ann Apartment Motel   2901 Belmar Street; (305) 565-5558. 15 units.
Quality Inn Oceanside   1208 North Ocean Boulevard, Pompano Beach; (305) 782-5300. 98 rooms.
Ramada Inn Oceanfront   4240 Galt Ocean Drive; (305) 566-8631. 94 rooms.
Ramada Inn Oceanfront of Hollywood Beach   2711 South Ocean Drive, Hollywood; (305) 922-8200 or toll free 1-800-2RAMADA. 198 rooms.
Sheraton Yankee Clipper   1140 Seabreeze Road; (305) 524-5551 or toll free 1-800-334-8484. 505 rooms.
Sheraton Yankee Trader   303 North Atlantic Boulevard; (305) 467-1111 or toll free 1-800-334-8484. 443 rooms.
Tiffany House   2900 Riomar Street; (305) 563-3116. 130 rooms.
Westin Cypress Creek   400 Corporate Drive; (305) 772-1331. 294 rooms.
Winterset   2801 Terramar Street; (305) 564-5614. 29 units.

MORSELS   Make room for this: there are more than 2500 restaurants listed in the phone book (more restaurants per capita than any other city in the country). The assortment includes some three dozen Chinese restaurants alone! The following are all located in the city:
Andrews Riverside Bar & Grill   2 South New River Drive W.; (305) 763-7911. Gourmet seafood. Situated on the New River.
Bobby Rubino's Place for Ribs   4100 North Federal Highway; (305) 561-5305. Barbecued ribs, chicken, and onion ring loaves.
Carlos and Pepe's Cantina   1302 Southeast 17th Street; (305) 467-7192. Mexican and American cuisine.
The Caves Restaurant   2205 North Federal Highway; (305) 561-4622. Continental dining in intimate, individual grottoes.
Chiang Mai of Siam   3341 North Federal Highway; (305) 565-0855. Thai food from authentic recipes.
Fifteenth Street Fisheries   1900 Southeast 15th Street (at Ft. Lauderdale Marina); (305) 763-2777. Fresh seafood.
Ft. Lauderdale Brauhaus Restaurant   1701 East Sunrise Boulevard; (305) 764-4104. German menu, steak, and seafood.

Frankie's 3333 Northeast 32nd Avenue; (305) 566-7853. Italian-American food, with emphasis on veal.

French Quarter Las Olas and Southeast 8th Avenue; (305) 467-2900. New Orleans and French dishes served up in an elegant atmosphere.

Il Giardino's 609 Las Olas Boulevard; (305) 763-3733. Northern Italian cuisine. The pasta's homemade.

Lagniappe Cajun House 230 East Las Olas Boulevard; (305) 467-7500. Cajun specialties. Brunch served Saturday and Sunday.

La Perla 1818 East Sunrise Boulevard; (305) 765-1950. Italian cooking, fine wines. Reservations requested.

Le Jardin Restaurant 2699 Stirling Road; (305) 966-7740. French cuisine.

Luigi's Italian Seafood House 563 West Oakland Park Boulevard; (305) 561-3322. Italian-American dishes, plus fresh seafood.

Mai-Kai 3599 North Federal Highway; (305) 563-3272. Cantonese and American menu. Nightly Polynesian shows.

Ruth's Chris Steak House 2525 North Federal Highway; (305) 565-2338. Varied menu, with steaks the specialty.

Shirttail Charlie's 400 Southwest 3rd Avenue; (305) 463-FISH. Fresh seafood.

The Spiced Apple 3281 Griffen Road; (305) 962-0772. Country and seafood specials. The *Miami Herald* gives this restaurant a four-star rating.

Vie de France Café/Bakery 2342-AE Sunrise Boulevard (at the Galleria); (305) 565-7544. Light menu, quiche, croissants, and soups. Also, fresh-baked goods.

Who Song and Larry's 3100 North Federal Highway; (305) 566-9771. Featured on the menu are Mexican and American dishes, barbecued ribs, chicken, and seafood.

ATTRACTIONS Downtown Ft. Lauderdale is clean, white, and vibrant. You'll find lots of shopping, historic sites, and parks. A walking tour of downtown can be covered in three hours. The chamber of commerce has a brochure that lets you guide yourself.

The Strip The infamous Strip (popularized in the movie *Where the Boys Are*) runs off East Las Olas Boulevard. The Strip accommodates revelers with a slew of bars, nightclubs, dives, joints, and hangouts. Be aware, also, of something called "The New Strip" on Commercial Boulevard. The locals call it "Magic Boulevard" because you are virtually guaranteed of going into any bar alone and coming out with a

IT'S YOUR CALL

Do broadcasters go through a spring training period of their own? The answer is yes.

"I've often remarked that the toughest games you do all year are the ones you do first, in spring training. When you haven't been broadcasting for a while, and you find yourself doing a spring game, with seventeen guys in the lineup, it's really tough. Plus, your team is playing teams in the other league, and you're not as familiar with their rosters, no matter how much homework you do. So, yeah, we work extremely hard in spring training."
—Andy Musser, broadcaster, Phillies

"Spring training gives us a chance to get refreshed on how to keep score, on how to keep balls and strikes, to realign yourself with what it's like to watch a game from the booth.

"In spring games, you interpret things a bit differently than you would in the regular season, when wins and losses are the bottom line. In the spring, you pay more attention to individual performances, maybe doing a little more interpreting of what a person's individual performance might mean. For example, how someone's coming off an arm injury. You pay attention to how he's throwing, and not so much whether he pitches three score-less innings. In the regular season, you're concerned with the final result: winning or losing.

"In spring training, you need to work harder. You have almost twice as many players as you do in the regular season, many of whom you are not familiar with. You have to study the nonroster players, the rookies. Because when they get into ball-games, people are wondering who they are. So you have a lot more players to be concerned about, not only on your own team, but the other team, too."
—Joe Castiglione, broadcaster, Red Sox

companion. There's more scoring on the Magic Strip than at a week's worth of action in the grapefruit league.

Air Boat Tours Located at Everglades Holiday Park at Griffin Road and U.S. 27 (21940 Griffin Road); (305) 434-8111. Tours of the Everglades are conducted by knowledgeable guides aboard the world's largest air boat.

Flamingo Gardens Located twelve miles west of town on State Road 84 at Flamingo Road; (305) 473-0010. The gardens include jungle hammocks, a mile-long tram ride, Gator World, botanical gardens, and an Everglades museum. Open daily, 9:00 A.M. to 5:00 P.M.

International Swimming Hall of Fame Located on the Intracoastal Highway off A1A; (305) 462-6536. The museum houses the world's most complete collection of swimming-related lore and memorabilia: exhibits, photos, medals, films, and a 5000-book library. Open daily.

Jungle Queen This three-hour cruise leaves from Bahia Mar at 10:00 A.M. and 2:00 P.M. The evening run at 7:00 P.M. includes a barbecue and shrimp dinner. Reservations required. Call (305) 462-5596.

Ocean World Located next to Marriott Hotel on Southeast 17th Street; (305) 525-6611. Aquatic shows with trained dolphins and sea lions. The kids will love the dolphin petting zoo. Open at 10:00 A.M. daily, the year round.

Paddlewheel Queen 2950 Northeast 32nd Avenue; (305) 564-7659. Enjoy a starlight dinner cruise, departing 7:30 P.M. and returning at 10:30 P.M. Dresses or dressy pantsuits required for women, sport jackets or dressy shirts for men (ties optional). No shorts, cutoffs, or T-shirts.

Six Flags Atlantis Water park located at 2700 Stirling Road, Hollywood; (305) 926-1000. Water slides, wave pool, shows, restaurants, shops.

Voyager Sightseeing Train located on the beach at 600 South Seabreeze and A1A; (305) 463-0401. The train gives you an eighteen-mile tour of Ft. Lauderdale and Port Everglades.

Events There are a number of events held in March. Call the chamber of commerce for exact dates. The festivals include the billfish tournament, a seafood festival, the Week of the Ocean celebration, the Opera Guild's opera series, and the Wilton Manors Tennis Classic.

Sports There are a number of city parks. Also, consider jai alai at Dania Jai Alai, U.S. 1 and Dania Beach Boulevard in Dania. Call (305) 945-4345. There are over fifty golf courses to choose from, and some 500 tennis courts. Call the chamber of commerce for information. And as you will find in any Florida beach haven, there's an assortment of fishing, swimming, boating, and diving opportunities.

Buehler Planetarium Located at Broward Community College; (305) 475-6680. Public shows are scheduled Thursdays at 7:30 P.M. and Sundays at 2:30 and 3:30 P.M.

Museum of Art Located at One East Las Olas Boulevard; (305) 525-5500. Permanent and changing exhibits. Closed Mondays.

Philharmonic Orchestra of Florida Performs classical and pop concerts in Broward and Palm Beach counties. Office located at 1430 North Federal Highway; (305) 392-7230.

There are several large shopping malls in the area. The largest are Broward Mall, University Drive and Broward Boulevard; Galleria, East Sunrise at Bayview; Hollywood Fashion Center, State Road and Hollywood Boulevard; Las Olas Boulevard, a street of shopping from Federal Highway to a block east of the Himmarshee Canal; and Pompano Fashion Square, off Federal Highway in Pompano Beach.

For more information, contact:
Greater Ft. Lauderdale Chamber of Commerce
208 Southeast Third Avenue
P.O. Box 14516
Ft. Lauderdale 33302
(305) 462-6000

Miami

BALTIMORE ORIOLES

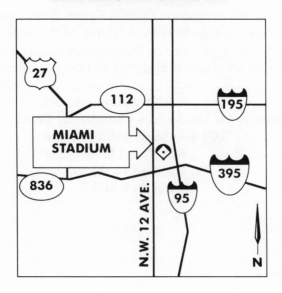

THE TEAM

The Orioles have trained exclusively in Miami since 1959, becoming as much a part of the Miami landscape as palm trees and Don Johnson's stubble. That's a long time for any team, but especially for the Orioles, since they came into existence as recently as 1954 (carrying on with the old St. Louis Browns franchise).

TEAM HOTEL   Hyatt Regency, 400 Southeast Second Avenue, Miami 33131; (305) 358-1234.

MIAMI STADIUM   Located a short distance away from the Orange Bowl, games in Miami Stadium are a little different from those in most Florida towns. One factor is the many night games the Orioles play. Many teams will not play a single spring home game at night; the Orioles will play close to half its home schedule under the lights.

With a game time of 7:30 P.M., plus the length of spring training games (usually approaching three hours with all the substitutions), it makes for a long night. Another difference is the size of Miami. It is a major metropolitan area, with the same problems that afflict many of our nation's large cities. A night game in these surroundings is something quite different than, say, an afternoon game in quiet Winter Haven.

Still another difference is the stadium itself, which is one of the biggest of all spring training parks. The permanent capacity of Miami Stadium is 9548, though the team will average around 4000. The record crowd is 12,464 for a game between Baltimore and the Yankees on March 14, 1965. While the size is not cavernous compared to major league parks, it does have a hollow feeling when you're sitting there with 6000 empty seats.

Pitchers and catchers report around February 21, with the rest of the team due usually on the last day of the month. Grapefruit action usually begins on or about March 7. Before the spring schedule starts, the team works out daily at the stadium beginning at 10:00 A.M. Workouts are free to the public.

An interesting thing is happening to Baltimore. They're having a harder and harder time coming up with a full spring schedule. The reason is that most of the teams that train in Florida are located in the center of the state or on the west coast, a long haul from Miami.

Add to that the fact that the Rangers moved from nearby Pompano to Port Charlotte in 1987, and what you get is a team more and more isolated. This isolation was one of the main reasons that the Royals moved out of Ft. Meyers after 1987, and it could happen to Baltimore.

Ticket prices are $7 for field boxes, $5 for terrace boxes, and $4 for general admission. Children and senior citizens can buy general admission tickets for just $2. For ticket information, call (305) 635-5395. **Address and Phone**   Miami Stadium, 2301 Northwest Tenth Avenue, Miami 33127; (305) 633-9857.

THE AREA

Miami, with a population of almost 2 million, is probably the most "visible" of all Florida towns. Jackie Gleason did his show from Miami for many years, and recently, "Miami Vice" has made the town a house-hold word. Another big draw is the Doral Open, held each March on the 6939-yard Doral Country Club Blue Course.

Miami is miles of beaches, tropical weather, a night life that cooks, and a city of cultural sophistication. But it's also a city with major problems. These include urban growth that's destroying precious wet-lands, racial unrest, drug trafficking. Still, on the whole, the Miami area is an exciting, fun spot for a spring vacation.

BEDDING DOWN There are about 60,000 hotel and motel rooms available in the greater Miami area, with all the major chains represent-ed. You'll find every type of accommodation you can think of, from a luxury penthouse to a single motel room. The majority of hotels and motels are concentrated along the beaches, downtown, and near the airport. In the better lodgings, the hotel concierge can give you recom-mendations for sightseeing, shopping, dining, and entertainment.

The following establishments are in Miami, unless otherwise noted:

The Biltmore Hotel 1200 Anastasia Avenue, Coral Gables; (305) 445-1926 or toll free 1-800-445-2586. Beautifully restored to its 1926 elegance, it's perfect for those who have the budget and the desire for something a little special.

The Bentley Hotel Ocean Drive at Fifth Avenue; (305) 538-1700. Oceanfront lodging with special introductory prices.

Art Deco Hotel Ocean Drive at 13th Street, Miami Beach; (305) 534-2135 or toll free 1-800-327-6306. Restored to 1930s origins.

Omni International Hotel 1601 Biscayne Boulevard; (305) 374-0000. 535 rooms in a luxury hotel, with fine restaurants and great service.

DuPont Plaza Hotel 300 Biscayne Boulevard; (305) 358-2541 or toll free 1-800-327-3480. 300 rooms.

Howard Johnson's Motor Lodge 1100 Biscayne Boulevard; (305) 358-3080. 115 rooms.

Mardi Gras Motel Apartments 3400 Biscayne Boulevard; (305) 573-7700. 50 units.

Marriott Hotel 1201 Northwest LeJeune Road; (305) 649-5000 or toll free 1-800-228-9290. 552 rooms.

Miami International Airport Hotel Northwest 20th Street at LeJeune Road; (305) 871-4100 or toll free 1-800-327-1276. 270 rooms.

Miami Miramar Hotel 1744 North Bayshore Drive; (305) 379-1865. 70 rooms.

Fontainbleau Hilton   4441 Collins Avenue, Miami Beach; (305) 538-2000. 1124 rooms, with legend to boot.

Hawaiian Isle Beach Resort   17601 Collins Avenue, Miami Beach; (305) 932-2121 or toll free 1-800-327-5275. 210 rooms.

Holiday Inn Hotel   8701 Collins Avenue, Miami Beach; (305) 866-5731. 216 rooms.

Sahara Resort Motel   18335 Collins Avenue, Miami Beach; (305) 931-8335 or toll free 1-800-432-2171. 144 rooms.

Thunderbird Resort Hotel   18401 Collins Avenue, Miami Beach; (305) 931-7700 or toll free 1-800-327-2044. 180 rooms.

Quality Inn Airport   1850 Northwest 42nd Avenue; (305) 871-4350 or toll free 1-800-228-5151. 216 rooms.

Ramada Inn   3941 Northwest 22nd Street; (305) 871-1700 or toll free 1-800-228-2828. 272 rooms.

Sheraton Royal Biscayne   555 Ocean Drive; (305) 361-5775 or toll free 1-800-325-3535. 194 rooms.

Silver Sands Motel   301 Ocean Drive; (305) 361-5441. Efficiencies and apartments.

Tarleton Hotel   2469 Collins Avenue, Miami Beach; (305) 538-5721 or toll free 1-800-327-3110. 80 rooms.

Town and Country Apartment Hotel   600 Coral Way, Coral Gables; (305) 444-6221. 20 apartments.

Sonesta Beach Hotel   350 Ocean Drive, Key Biscayne; (305) 361-2021 or toll free 1-800-343-7170. 293 rooms.

MORSELS   Miami is truly a world-class restaurant city. These restaurants are in Miami, unless otherwise noted:

Shooters on the Water   3969 Northeast 163rd Street, North Miami Beach; (305) 949-2855. Shrimp, potato skins, fish of the day, prime rib. Patio dining on the waterfront.

Tony Roma's   2665 Southwest 37th Avenue; (305) 443-6626. Ribs served in heaping portions. Menu includes chicken, pork, and beef.

New York Steak House   17985 Biscayne Boulevard, North Miami Beach; (305) 932-7676. Specialty is hand-aged prime steaks. Also served are Maine lobsters, jumbo stone crabs, and fresh fish.

Place for Steak   1335 79th Street Causeway, Miami Beach; (305) 758-5581. One of the city's oldest steak houses, serving prime quality beef. Live entertainment.

Wong's Shanghai Restaurant   17953 West Dixie Highway, North

A STAR IS BORN

Outside of Miami Stadium, the Orioles had parking spaces reserved for the press. On the block in front, it would have a small sign saying 'Reserved for *Baltimore Sun*' or 'Reserved for the *News-American*.' At that time (in the late sixties and early seventies), the team would get coverage from some of the Central American papers, since Miami was so close to Cuba and Nicaragua. And there was a sign reserving a parking space for the *Cuban Star* newspaper. That's what the sign said: '*Cuban Star*.' Mike Cuellar, who was then a star pitcher for the Birds, would always park his car in that space. He would say 'That's me . . . Cuban star.' "

—Dan Shaughnessy, *Boston Globe* and former Baltimore baseball writer

Miami Beach; (305) 949-4944. Mandarin, Szechuan, Hunan, and Cantonese cuisine.

Yeung's Gardens 1211 71st Street, Miami Beach; (305) 868-1211. Cantonese cooking, generous portions.

Charade 2900 Ponce de León Boulevard, Coral Gables; (305) 448-6077. Located in a landmark Spanish building, Charade's offers a full continental menu.

Dining Galleries—Fontainbleau 4441 Collins Avenue, Miami Beach; (305) 538-2000. This is truly a world-class experience. The award-winning menu features continental cuisine.

Padrino's 2500 East Hallandale Beach Boulevard, Hallandale; (305) 456-4550. Home-cooked Cuban food. Specialties include roast pork and breaded steak.

Tivoli 3439 Sunny Isles Boulevard (Northeast 163rd Street), North Miami Beach; (305) 945-7080. Danish cooking. Specials include roast duck and veal oscar.

Dominique's 5225 Collins Avenue (at Alexander Hotel), Miami Beach; (305) 861-5252. French cuisine, imported dover sole, roasted quail, and mallard duck flown in fresh daily.

Café Chauveron 9561 East Bay Harbor Drive, Bay Harbor; (305) 866-8779. Haute cuisine, French provincial. Jackets required.

Csarda 13885 Biscayne Boulevard; (305) 940-1095. Full Hungarian menu.

Café Tanino 2312 Ponce de León Boulevard, Coral Gables; (305) 446-1666. Northern Italian cuisine, serving homemade pasta.

San Remo 4300 Collins Avenue, Miami Beach; (305) 531-4159. Specialties from northern Italy. All pastas and desserts made on the premises.

Pappagallo 11500 Biscayne Boulevard, North Miami; (305) 895-3730. A small, intimate place serving up veal, beef, fish, chicken, and pasta.

Masa-San 19355 Northwest Second Avenue (U.S. 441), North Miami Beach; (305) 651-7782. Japanese cuisine served either tempura or teriyaki style. Large sushi bar.

Crab House 1551 79th Street Causeway, North Bay Village; (305) 868-7085. Located on Biscayne Bay, with a huge seafood menu. Tip: try the garlic crabs.

Joe's Stone Crab 227 Biscayne Street, Miami Beach; (305) 673-0365. Stone crabs, unusual vegetables, and prime steaks.

Mike Gordon's 1201 79th Street Causeway; (305) 751-4429. Maine lobster, red snapper, stone crabs, oysters.

Joe's Seafood   400-404 Northwest North River Drive; (305) 374-5637. Seafood delicacies at moderate prices.

ATTRACTIONS   The main attraction in the Miami area is probably the beach, so here's a listing of them:

Lummus Park   6th Street to 14th Street on Miami Beach. Plenty of palm trees for shade. Lifeguards. Meter parking.

35th Street and 21st Street Beach   Small, convenient beaches with wooden boardwalk. Lifeguards.

53rd Street and 63rd Street Beach   On Miami Beach. Two small beaches between hotels. Lifeguards and rest rooms.

72nd-74th Street Beach   Along Oceanfront on Miami Beach. Shaded beach, lifeguards, municipal parking.

Northshore Open Space Park Beach   From 79th Street to 87th Street along A1A on Miami Beach. Wooden boardwalks, wooden roofed pavilions, and exercise course with twenty stations. Rest rooms and lifeguards.

Surfside Beach   88th Street to 96th Street, in the town of Surfside. Public parking, lifeguard station.

Haulover Beach   Between Bal Harbour and Motel Row. Picnic facilities, barbecue grilles, snack bar, fishing pier, rest rooms, and lifeguards.

Crandon Park Beach   Key Biscayne. Two-mile beach, miniature golf course, amusement park, picnic area, lifeguards.

Virginia Beach   Off Rickenbacker Causeway, Key Biscayne. This is a rugged, less developed beach, with lifeguards on duty weekends and holidays only. But because it's not developed, the chance for privacy is better here.

Sports include golf, tennis, fishing, boating, swimming, jai alai, greyhound racing, horse shows, soccer, regattas, bicycling, and water sports such as scuba, snorkeling, surfing, and windsurfing.

Art Deco District   Miami Beach; (305) 672-2014. From 6th to 23rd streets between Jefferson Avenue and the beach, there are more than 800 buildings done in the Art Deco style of the 1930s. Guided tours given each Saturday morning at 10:30 A.M. for $5 per person.

Cauley Square Village Shops   22400 Old Dixie Highway; (305) 258-3543. This area of shops and boutiques is in a converted ten-acre railroad village.

Fairchild Tropical Gardens   10901 Old Cutler Road, Coral Gables; (305) 667-1651. This is the largest botanical garden in the country, with eight lakes, a rain forest, sunken gardens, and a rare-plant house. Open daily from 9:30 A.M. to 4:30 P.M.

Fruit and Spice Park   24801 Southwest 187th Avenue, Homestead; (305) 247-5727. Twenty-acre botanical garden with hundreds of species of fruit, nuts, and spices. Featured on ABC's "Good Morning America."

Metro-Dade Cultural Center   101 West Flagler Street; (305) 375-1700. This fine complex includes the Center for the Fine Arts, the Historical Museum of Southern Florida, and the Miami-Dade Public Library.

Miami Metrozoo   Coral Reef Drive (Southwest 152nd Street) and Southwest 124th Street (just west of the turnpike exit); (305) 251-0401. This cageless zoo represents the latest in modern zoo design. More than one hundred species of animals roam free in 225 acres of land. Also included are elephant rides, a petting zoo, boat rides, viewing roads, walking tours, and outdoor concert series.

Museum of Science and Space Travel Planetarium   3280 South Miami Avenue; (305) 854-4247. More than one hundred hands-on exhibits dealing with light, sound, electronics, electricity, biology, and energy. Open daily from 10:00 A.M. to 6:00 P.M.

Spanish Monastery   16711 West Dixie Highway, North Miami Beach; (305) 945-1461. This is the oldest building in the Western Hemisphere. First erected in Spain in 1141, it was dismantled and brought to Miami in 1954. Now houses art and antiques.

Miami also abounds in museums, galleries, performing arts (theater, music, dance), and film. Write or call the chamber of commerce for more information.

And if you have time, explore Little Havana between downtown Miami on the east and Coral Gables. The area features boutiques, shops, restaurants, and a cosmopolitan atmosphere.

For more information, contact:
Greater Miami Chamber of Commerce
1601 Biscayne Boulevard
Miami 33132
(305) 350-7700

Port St. Lucie

NEW YORK METS

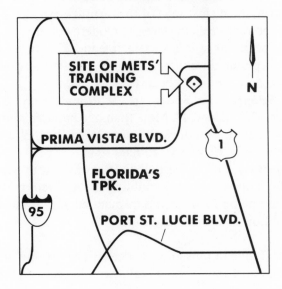

THE TEAM

Following the spring of 1987, the Mets severed their long-standing relationship with St. Petersburg and moved across state to the east coast and Port St. Lucie.

The Mets have built a state-of-the-park spring training facility in this little town south of Vero Beach between Ft. Pierce (ten miles to the north) and Stuart (ten miles to the south).

The complex, dedicated in the spring of 1988, features six practice fields, an air-conditioned clubhouse, and a 7500-seat stadium over a one-hundred-acre site.

In the fall, the Mets will use the facility for instructional baseball for its minor leaguers. The spring training facility—which will consolidate the entire Mets operation, both major and minor, under one roof—is located in St. Lucie West.

ST. LUCIE WEST Construction on this city within a city began in April 1986. The development consists of 7 square miles of land directly west of north Port St. Lucie. You can reach the site by car by taking Prima Vista Boulevard or by an overpass over the Florida Turnpike. The Mets complex is actually west of U.S. 1.

St. Lucie West, which includes the Mets complex, is a totally planned community, with construction slated through the 1990s. By the year 2000, it is expected that about 85 percent of the following facilities will be in place (the Mets, of course, will be playing ball there by 1988):

- some 15,000 dwellings, with a population of about 36,000, a figure based on the current rate of 2.5 persons per dwelling in Port St. Lucie
- more than 1000 hotel/motel rooms
- about 1.4 million square feet of commercial space including outparcels
- 4 golf courses
- 2 universities
- 6 million square feet of space for light industry
- and a partridge in a palm tree

The Mets training facility places it close to the Dodgers at Vero Beach to the north and within a relatively easy drive to the Braves and Expos camps in West Palm Beach, the Yankees in Ft. Lauderdale, and the Orioles in Miami.

For complete information on the Mets facility, including ticket prices, spring schedule, and so on, contact either the Port St. Lucie Chamber of Commerce or the Mets PR office in New York at (718) 507-6387, or write the Mets at Shea Stadium, Flushing, NY 11368.

THE AREA

Just a couple of decades ago, Port St. Lucie bore little resemblance to what it is, and what it is becoming, today. The land was wide open and undeveloped, except for a few orange groves. Today, the word is "growth." In the 1980 census, the population was 14,690; today, it's approaching 40,000.

IT'S SPRING OF A DIFFERENT NATURE

A couple of big changes in spring training today compared to years ago have to do with the minor league organizations and breaking camp.

The trend today is for clubs to have their entire operations in the same city, usually at one complex, as is the case with the Mets in Port St. Lucie. Years ago, this was different, mainly because of the size of the minor leagues. Teams would have a proliferation of clubs in many different leagues. The hundreds of ball players in an organization presented certain logistical problems, almost all reducing to a sheer problem of numbers.

For example, when the Red Sox moved to Winter Haven in 1966, their minor league operation was some ninety miles away in Ocala. But with fewer minor league teams, clubs are trying to get everyone under one roof.

Breaking camp is another difference. From the first years of spring training, on through the fifties and sixties, teams would traditionally break camp early and work their way north, instead of staying in camp until the day before the regular season begins, as is done today.

For example, the Cleveland Indians of 1955 broke camp in Tuscon, Arizona, when the New York Giants broke theirs in Phoenix: about three weeks before opening day. The two teams, who played each other in the World Series the autumn before, then barnstormed throughout the South and on the way north. They played each other in a series of games in towns such as Wichita Falls, Texas; Paris, Texas; Shreveport, Louisiana; New Orleans; and numerous other small southern towns.

Clubs would travel by train. Players would suit up on the train as it pulled into town. They'd play the game, come back in uniforms, then undress and shower on the train. Players bunked with each other in roomettes. With lots of travel and little else to do, there was great camaraderie. The clubs were actually like a big band doing a series of one-night stands.

One of the most surprising statistics of the city is the median age. Take a guess. Did you say sixty-five? Sixty-two? You weren't even close. It's thirty-eight.

Located on the southeast coast, Port St. Lucie is 110 miles north of Miami, and 50 miles north of West Palm Beach. The climate leads to year-round outdoor recreation, with March being the most popular tourist month. The terrain, as it is in almost all of Florida, is flat, with an average elevation of a mere five feet above sea level (five inches shorter than Fred Patek). There are lots of streams, and two rivers run through the city: the Indian River and the St. Lucie River. In the developed portions of the region, the rivers spin off into side channels, which lend character to the residential neighborhoods.

BEDDING DOWN   With the influx of commercial growth, to say nothing of the impact the Mets will have on the area, hotel and motel space is being built at a furious pace. Many major chains are expected to build in the area. One hotel under construction and expected to be ready by spring training 1988 is the Best Western. The hotel site is on Route 1, outside of Spanish Lakes, a mobile home community.

To obtain the most complete and up-to-date listings of hotel and motel space, write or call the chamber of commerce.

Outrigger Resort   1405 Northeast Indian River Drive, Jensen Beach; (305) 287-2411.

You can also check out accommodations in White Beach, Stuart, or Ft. Pierce.

MORSELS   Again, check with the area chamber of commerce for the most up-to-date listings, as new restaurants will be going up for the next several years.

Dino's Pizza   1002 Southeast Port St. Lucie Boulevard, Port St. Lucie; (305) 335-3466.

Easy Street Restaurant and Lounge   1034 Southeast Port St. Lucie Boulevard; Port St. Lucie; (305) 335-4433.

La Bella Napoli   1145 Port St. Lucie Boulevard; Port St. Lucie; (305) 335-5303. Family restaurant and pizzeria, cocktail lounge.

Golden Dragon Restaurant and Lounge   10044 South U.S. 1, Port St. Lucie; (305) 335-8051. Chinese cuisine.

Johnny's Corner   7992 South U.S. 1, Port St. Lucie; (305) 878-2686.

Mr. Laff's Riverfront Restaurant   2075 Northeast Indian River Drive, Jensen Beach; (305) 334-3000.
Outrigger Resort and Restaurant   1405 Northeast Indian River Drive, Jensen Beach; (305) 287-2411.
Palermo's Restaurant and Pizzeria   7123 South U.S. 1, Port St. Lucie; (305) 878-2800.
Port St. Lucie Country Treat   6721 South U.S. 1, Port St. Lucie; (305) 461-4363.

ATTRACTIONS   With the newness of the Mets facility and because there's a fascination one always finds with the "new," for the "new" is unexplored, you might be spending more time at the park than you normally would. But even allowing for that, you'll have plenty of ways to fill your other time (i.e., your nonbaseball time) in Port St. Lucie.
Fort Pierce Jai Alai   They call it world's fastest ball game, and when you see what its players do with the hard ball that ricochets around the court at 175 mph, either you'll wonder if their elevators go up to the top floor or you'll be hooked. Pari-mutuel betting adds to the excitement, though adding to jai alai's excitement is like putting Tabasco sauce on red pepper. The season begins in March and runs through the middle of September. Game time is 7:00 P.M. Monday, Wednesday, Friday, and Saturday. Dinner reservations are accepted. Located one mile north of the Fort Pierce exit (#56) of the Florida Turnpike. For information, call (305) 464-7500.
St. Lucie County Historical Museum   One of the best buys in all Florida, with admission only $1 (50 cents for kids). Exhibits include a restored Spanish galleon sunk by a 1715 hurricane. There are also military artifacts from Fort Pierce, built in 1838 in the Seminole War (1835–1842). "Living history" demonstrations are included. Open Wednesday through Sunday from 10:00 A.M. to 4:00 P.M.
UDT-SEAL Frogman Museum   The theme of this collection is the Navy's elite Underwater Demolition Teams (UDTs) and Sea, Air, and Land (SEAL) teams active in World War II. Displays include documents, artifacts, photographs, and paintings from World War II, Korea, and Vietnam. The museum is at 414 Seaway Drive in Pepper State Park on north Hutchinson Island (north of Fort Pierce inlet). Information: (305) 464-FROG.
Treasure Coast Children's Museum   Situated in the Monterey Shopping Center, Stuart. The museum displays model trains, exercise exhibits, a racing go-cart, a teaching computer, and a wild room of mirrors

that create a psychedelic effect by multiplying the image of the child many times. The great thing about this place is that it allows kids to let off some energy. Information: (305) 286-1333.

St. Lucie County Civic Center This facility presents a variety of entertainment throughout the year, from concerts, to dog shows, to ballet. To check on the bill and for reservations and ticket information, call (305) 466-1100.

The Treasure Coast Symphony A fine orchestral group that presents concerts at the Fort Pierce Jai Alai Fronton. Information: (305) 464-2671 or 465-5264. The symphony's mailing address is TCS, P.O. Box 4169, Fort Pierce 33448.

The Barn Theater A talented amateur theater located at 2400 East Ocean Boulevard, Stuart; (305) 287-4884.

St. Lucie Community Theater Just north of Port St. Lucie at 629 Weatherbee Road, Fort Pierce; (305) 878-4199.

Sea Turtle Rookery Sea turtles use the beaches of the Atlantic for nesting sites. This one is located on the south end of Hutchinson Island. Many of the turtles you'll see, including the Atlantic Green Turtle, Loggerheads, and Leatherbacks, are endangered species and are protected. *Do not* touch, molest, bother, poach, destroy, or in any way interfere with the turtles, their nests, or their eggs. This action will be met by a heavy fine or prison, and maybe both. Also, don't take dogs with you to see this fascinating site. And keep the noise down. You'll be rewarded with a unique experience.

House of Refuge This museum is one of the area's oldest buildings, built in 1875 (as a refuge for shipwrecked sailors). Exhibits include early life-saving equipment, maritime artifacts, souvenirs, and home furnishings from the late Victorian era. Open 1:00 to 5:00 P.M. Tuesday through Sunday. Information: (305) 224-1875.

Golf courses include Sandpiper Bay, Village Hotel. Public tennis courts include Sportsmen's Park and Lyngate Park (Lyngate is open at night also).

Public parks offer many activities, including tennis, baseball, basketball, running, exercise trails, fishing, picnic tables, and playgrounds. Contact the Port St. Lucie Recreation Department for more information.

With the Atlantic Ocean just minutes away, and with a number of freshwater lakes and ponds, opportunities for boating and fishing are great. Saltwater fishing is found in the Indian River (spotted sea trout is the most popular fish), Hutchinson Island, and offshore from the St. Lucie inlet. Freshwater action can be found at area ponds, canals, and the St. Lucie River, as well as at nearby lakes. Leisurely fishing can be had on the causeways in Stuart and Jensen Beach. Canoeing and sailing are fun, but if you're not familiar with the Atlantic waters, stay on the rivers . . . storms come up quickly over the ocean.

For more information, contact:
The Greater Port St. Lucie Chamber of Commerce
1626 Southeast Port St. Lucie Boulevard
Port St. Lucie 33452
(305) 335-4422

Vero Beach

LOS ANGELES DODGERS

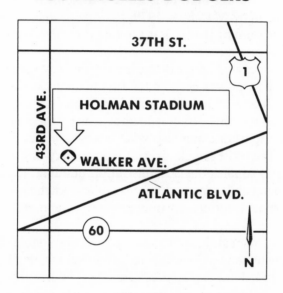

THE TEAM

The Dodgers have trained at the aptly-named Dodgertown since 1948 when businessman Bud Holman (for whom the stadium is named) invited the team to train in Vero Beach. Holman got his idea after World War II, when the Feds turned over a naval air training station to the city. The city needed a tenant, the club needed a camp. As a result, Vero Beach is the smallest city in America (population 16,000) to host a major league team.

Dodgertown is the only privately owned baseball training camp in the country. Walter and Peter O'Malley developed the facility, which now includes Holman Stadium, three practice fields, a gallery of batting cages, four practice pitching mounds, a sliding pit, and even a rundown track (no, not for players who are feeling tired, but for baserunning drills).

TEAM HOTEL The team stays on site at Dodgertown, 3901 26th Street, Vero Beach 32960; (305) 569-4900.

HOLMAN STADIUM Holman is a comfortable park with great seats. The stadium was built in 1953. It seats some 6000 fans, though 8200 squeezed in on March 19, 1979, for a game against the Yankees. An unusual feature of the park is the fact that there's no center field fence. There's just a rope.

The facility began a trend that changed the way spring training is conducted. The Dodgers became the first team in baseball to have its major and minor league teams train in the same location.

Dodgertown has changed considerably since its inception, growing from a rather spartan camp into what is now a major resort facility.

Replacing the old barracks is a modern ninety-unit villa, built in 1976. A 23,000-square-foot administration building was constructed in 1974, housing clubhouses, dining room and kitchen, a medical department, trainers' rooms, an interview room, and even a recording studio.

In addition, recreation and meeting facilities enable the 450-acre complex to be rented out privately to businesses for meetings and conferences. Included are two eighteen-hole golf courses (complete with clubhouse), a swimming pool, four tennis courts, a movie theater, and conference space. There are twelve meeting rooms fully equipped with audiovisual gear. Dodgertown can handle up to 180 conferees.

In the summer, Holman Stadium is home of the Vero Beach Dodgers of the Florida State League. For those who are interested, Dodgertown is a year-round operation that employs 250 persons and pays a local tax tab of $160,000 (about three weeks of Fernando Valenzuela's pay).

Catchers and pitchers report around February 20, with the rest of the squad due some five days later. Workouts begin daily at 10:00 A.M. Exhibition games begin at 1:30 P.M.

Season tickets for exhibition games are sold until March 1. After that, tickets are sold for individual games only. All seats in Holman Stadium are reserved boxes, going for $6. Standing-room-only tickets, selling for $4, are available after the reserved box seats are sold out.

That happens frequently, by the way, with the Dodgers averaging about 6000 a game. So plan ahead and buy your tickets as soon as possible.

This isn't the only ticket action taking place at Holman Stadium. Each year at the stadium, the Dodgers sell more than 3000 season tickets for Los Angeles home games in L.A.

Address and Phone Dodgertown, 4001 26th Street, P.O. Box 2887, Vero Beach 32961; (305) 569-4900.

THE AREA

Vero Beach, midway down the state on the east coast of Florida, is a quiet little town that has always been popular as a year-round resort. Because the town is small, the beaches are relatively unspoiled and uncrowded.

BEDDING DOWN All of the following listings, which include both beach area and mainland, are in Vero Beach:

Capri Motel/Apartments 625 Royal Palm Boulevard; (305) 562-2910.

Citrus Motel 3256 U.S. 1; (305) 562-4163.

Days Inn of Vero Beach 8800 20th Street; (305) 562-9991.

Dolphin Motel 1850 U.S. 1; (305) 567-5349.

Drake Motel 2022 U.S. 1; (305) 567-4331.

Holiday Inn Countryside State Road 60 at I-95; (305) 567-8321.

Howard Johnson's Downtown 1725 U.S. 1; (305) 567-5171.

Landmark Motor Lodge 1706 U.S. 1; (305) 562-6591.

Rexton Inn 1985 90th Avenue; (305) 778-1985.

Tropical Palms Motel 746 18th Street; (305) 562-6764.

Aquarius Ocean Front Resort 1526 South Ocean Drive; (305) 231-5218.

Azalea Lane Apartments 897 Azalea Lane; (305) 231-4310.

Beachland Fountains 571 Beachland Boulevard; (305) 231-0101.

Beach Vue Motel 3005 Ocean Drive; (305) 231-6700.

Driftwood Inn Motel 3240 Ocean Drive; (305) 231-2800.

Holiday Inn Oceanside 3384 Ocean Drive; (305) 231-2300.

The Islander 3101 Ocean Drive; (305) 231-4431.

Pickett Suite Resort Hotel 3500 Ocean Drive; (305) 231-5666.

Riviera Inn 1601–1605 South Ocean Drive; (305) 234-4112.

Sea Spray Gardens 965 East Causeway Boulevard; (305) 231-5210.

Sea Vista Motel 1508 South Ocean Drive; (305) 231-5366.

THE DODGER TAIL WAGS THE VERO DOG

The question's been asked many times: just how important are the Dodgers to Vero Beach? From a financial standpoint, the Dodgers draw many fans—and their money—into the area. To that you must add what the club spends to run its camp (the team has a policy of trying whenever possible to buy locally), what it pays the city each year in property taxes ($160,000), and what it pays to the 250 employees of Dodgertown. The total is about $10 million.

Then there's the question of public relations. There's not a lot to do in Vero Beach . . . there's no major attraction in the league of Disney World or Boardwalk and Baseball amusement park. But there are the Dodgers, and each spring, for six weeks, news from the Dodger camp spreads the Vero Beach dateline all over the country. This generates interest in the community that no amount of money could buy through ad or PR campaigns. As a chamber of commerce executive remarked, without the Dodgers, "life would be boring."

Then there's the corporate aspect. When Dodgerland first opened, recreational facilities consisted of horseshoes and badminton, with no meeting rooms. Now, the complex is loaded with complete recreational and meeting facilities. As a result, Dodgertown is used year round by companies looking for an out-of-the-ordinary conference location.

It's almost literally true—especially given the fierce and sophisticated development of nearby Central Florida—without the Dodgers, Vero Beach would probably wither away.

MORSELS Unless otherwise indicated, the following restaurants are in Vero Beach:

Black Pearl Restaurant 1409 South A1A; (305) 231-7966.

Bobby's Café 1453 20th Street; (305) 569-7745.

The Charleston 575 Miracle Mile; (305) 569-1920.

Coco's 6260 North A1A; (305) 231-0702.

Days Inn Restaurant 8800 20th Street; (305) 562-9991.

Dodger Pines Country Club Walker Avenue; (305) 569-4400.

Enriqo's Mexican Kitchen 3215 South U.S. 1, Ft. Pierce; (305) 465-1608.

Forty One 41 Royal Palm Boulevard; (305) 562-1141.

Holiday Inn Oceanside 3384 Ocean Drive; (305) 231-2300.

Holiday Inn Countryside State Road 60 at I-95; (305) 567-8321.

Hong Sam 901 Miracle Mile; (305) 569-5434.

Houlihan's 398 21st Street; (305) 569-1522.

Keller's Fat Boy BBQ 1150 South U.S. 1; (305) 562-8333.

The Lemon Tree 3544 Ocean Drive; (305) 231-4000.

Lobster Shanty 1 Royal Palm Boulevard; (305) 562-1941.

Mama Mia's Italian Restaurant 7401 U.S. 1; (305) 569-0120.

Maryland Fried Chicken 748 Miracle Mile; (305) 567-5360.

Mash Hoagies 4069 Ocean Drive; (305) 231-9436.

Morrison's Cafeteria Vero Mall on U.S. 1; (305) 569-3364.

Ocean Grille 1050 Sexton Plaza; (305) 231-5409.

Paisano's Pizza 'n Pasta 1605 U.S. 1; (305) 569-9777.

Patio Restaurant 1103 Miracle Mile; (305) 567-7215.

Silver Trivet Restaurant 2204 Miracle Mile; (305) 778-0815.

Sorrentino's Italian Restaurant North U.S. 1, Ft. Pierce; (305) 464-0011.

Summit Landings & Yachting Center 8524 North U.S. 1; (305) 589-3029.

Swenson's Ice Cream & Restaurant 1902 U.S. 1; (305) 569-9824.

Taco Viva 1266 U.S. 1; (305) 569-9586.

Uptown Restaurant 2023 14th Avenue; (305) 562-1302.

Village South 2900 Ocean Drive; (305) 231-6727.

Vincent's Pizza & Brew 2146 Miracle Mile; (305) 569-4333.

Wayside Inn 805 21st Street; (305) 562-6065.

Westside Beanery 4211 20th Street; (305) 562-0911.

Wright's Steak House 780 U.S. 1; (305) 562-9832.

ATTRACTIONS Vero Beach is a small town, with small town attractions.

Bingo   A big activity in town, seven days a week.

Sunday—1:45 P.M. at St. Helen's Social Hall, 2026 20th Street.

Monday—7:30 P.M. at the Elk's Lodge, 1359 26th Street.

Tuesday—7:00 P.M. at the American Legion Hall, 1749 Old Dixie.

Wednesday—7:30 P.M. at the Moose Lodge, 226 43rd Avenue.

Thursday—7:30 P.M. at the Italian American Club, 1600 25th Street.

Friday—1:00 P.M. at the VFW Post Hall, 2500 15th Avenue and 7:45 P.M. at St. Helen's Social Hall.

Saturday—7:45 P.M. at St. Helen's Social Hall.

Boating   Rentals at Vero Marine Center, 12 Royal Palm Boulevard.

Fishing   Deep-sea charters available in Ft. Pierce. Contact the Ft. Pierce Chamber of Commerce, 200 Virginia Avenue, (305) 464-2700.

Golf   There are three public courses in Vero Beach. Two are at Dodertown (Dodger Pines, eighteen holes and Dodgertown, nine holes). The third is Vista Plantation, State Road 60, eighteen holes.

Tennis   There are two public courts, one at Pocahontas Park, one-hour limit, first come, first served; the other is at Memorial Isles Tennis and Racquet Club, east end of Barber Bridge. Call (305) 231-4787 for reservations.

McLarty Museum   On North A1A. Fascinating displays of sunken treasures salvaged off the coast of Vero Beach. Open Wednesday through Sunday, 9:00 A.M. to 5:00 P.M. Admission 50 cents.

Vero Beach Theater Guild   2020 San Juan Avenue. Live entertainment. Call the chamber of commerce for more information.

In addition to the above, you can play shuffleboard on twenty-six championship courts in Pocahontas Park. There are eight playgrounds throughout the city and four parks along the beach. If surfing's your thing, try the waves at Conn Beach on Ocean Drive.

For more information, contact:
Vero Beach–Indian River Chamber of Commerce
1216 21st Street
P.O. Box 2947
Vero Beach 32961
(305) 567-3491

West Palm Beach

ATLANTA BRAVES AND
MONTREAL EXPOS

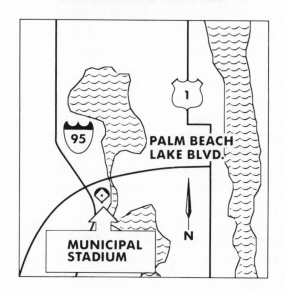

THE TEAMS

You'll double your pleasure and double your fun when you spend any part of a spring training getaway in West Palm Beach. The town hosts not one, but two ball clubs: the Braves and the Expos. The two clubs share Municipal Stadium, which means that once the grapefruit games begin, there's a game virtually every day for a month.

TEAM HOTELS Braves—Hyatt Palm Beaches, 630 Clearwater Park Road, West Palm Beach 33404; (305) 833-1234. Expos—Holiday Inn, 4431 PGA Boulevard, Palm Beach Gardens 33410; (305) 622-2260.

MUNICIPAL STADIUM This park, built by the city in 1963 when the Braves moved to West Palm Beach, seats 5000. As we said, the best part of Municipal during the spring is that there's a game almost every day. The two ball clubs coordinate their respective spring schedules so that while the Braves are at home, the Expos are on the road . . . except, of course, when the two teams play each other. Distances to the fences are 330 feet to left and right, 400 feet to center.

The teams have separate workout fields and facilities adjacent to the park. The Braves generally report earlier than most clubs, battery-men arriving on or about February 20, with the full squad on February 25. The Expos pitchers and catchers report around the 25th, with the full squad three days later. The Braves minor leaguers train in West Palm, reporting by March 9 or 10. Expos bushers play about ten miles south in Lantana, a speck on the map with no other claim to fame except that it's also home of the *National* (Dwarf Meter Maid, Abducted by Aliens, Gives Birth to Intelligent Coin Slot) *Enquirer.*

One unique thing about spring in West Palm: with the Expos in town, it brings a decidedly French-Canadian flavor to West Palm Beach. Game time for Braves games is 1:05 P.M. for afternoon contests, 7:05 P.M. for infrequent night games. The Expos play at 1:30 P.M. and 7:30 P.M., though night games are rare.

Tickets cost the same for both teams, with boxes at $7, reserved grandstand $6, and general admission $3. For complete ticket information, call the Municipal ticket office at (305) 689-9121.
Address and Phones Municipal Stadium, 715 Hank Aaron Drive, West Palm Beach 33404. Braves phone — (305) 683-6100. Expos phone — (305) 684-6801. Quickest way to the stadium is off I-95, exit 53, onto Palm Beach Lakes Boulevard East.

THE AREA

West Palm Beach is a small town in the general vicinity of an area known simply as the Palm Beaches. This includes Palm Beach, Tequesta, Jupiter, Juno, Singer Island, and West Palm Beach. The mention of this area invariably evokes thoughts and images of Palm Beach, *the* prime resort community, where cigars are lit with $50 bills and rolled with C notes. More on Palm Beach later.

Actually, Palm Beach is the largest Florida county, encompassing thirty-two communities. The Gulf Stream jets closer to the shores of the county than anywhere else on the Atlantic coastline, which accounts for both a magnificent tropical climate and some great fishing.

BEDDING DOWN   Most hotel chains have properties in Palm Beach County. Consult the Yellow Pages or write the chamber of commerce for complete listings.

Airport International Inn   1721 Belvedere Road, West Palm Beach; (305) 686-6700. 64 rooms.

Holiday Inn   6255 West Okeechobee Road, West Palm Beach; (305) 686-6000 or toll free 1-800-238-8000. 154 rooms.

Holiday Inn/West Palm Beach   100 Datura Street, West Palm Beach; (305) 655-8800 or toll free 1-800-238-8000. 165 rooms.

Palm Beach Polo & CC   13198 Forest Hill Boulevard, West Palm Beach; (305) 793-1113 or toll free 1-800-432-4151. 100 units.

Parkview Motor Lodge   4710 South Dixie, West Palm Beach; (305) 833-4644. 28 rooms.

Ramada Inn/Golf Course   1800 Palm Beach Lakes Boulevard, West Palm Beach; (305) 683-8810. 162 rooms.

Sheraton Inn/West Palm Beach   1901 West Palm Beach Lakes, West Palm Beach; toll free 1-800-325-3535. 157 rooms.

Tennis Club of Palm Beach   2800 Haverhill, West Palm Beach; (305) 683-6371. 35 rooms.

Beachcomber Apartment Motel   3024 South Ocean Boulevard, Palm Beach; (305) 585-4648. 40 rooms.

Brazilian Court Hotel   300 Brazilian Avenue, Palm Beach; (305) 655-7740. 125 rooms.

The Breakers Hotel   South County Road, Palm Beach; (305) 655-6611. 570 rooms. This five-star property is one regal expanse of Persian sofas, Venetian arches, and chandeliers. It may be the country's most stately first-class resort hotel.

Colony Hotel   155 Hammon Avenue, Palm Beach; (305) 655-5430. 100 rooms.

Heart Palm Beach Motor Inn   160 Royal Palm Way, Palm Beach; (305) 655-5600. 58 rooms.

Howard Johnson's Motor Lodge   2870 South County Road, Palm Beach; (305) 582-2581 or toll free 1-800-654-2000.

La Coquille Club   South Ocean Boulevard, Palm Beach; (305) 582-7411. 100 rooms.

Palm Beach Hilton   2842 South Ocean Boulevard, Palm Beach; (305) 586-6542. 134 rooms.

Palm Beach Ocean Hotel   2770–2830 Ocean Boulevard, Palm Beach; (305) 582-5381 or toll free 1-800-327-9407. 266 rooms.

Palm Beach Spa Hotel   337 Everglades Avenue, Palm Beach; (305) 833-8411. 200 rooms.

Testas Hotel   221 Royal Poinciana, Palm Beach; (305) 832-2672. 28 rooms.

MORSELS   The area offers some exciting dining experiences. Here are a few:

Café Palmiers   630 Clearwater Park (in the Hyatt Palm Beaches Hotel); (305) 833-1234. Continental menu, including fish and lamb, served in an elegant atmosphere. Sunday brunch 10:30 A.M. to 2:30 P.M. Reservations suggested.

Terrace   630 Clearwater Park (in the Hyatt Palm Beaches Hotel); (305) 833-1234. Breakfast, lunch, and dinner under skylights. Burgers, salads, entrées.

Musicana Dinner Theater   Two blocks west of Palm Beach Kennel Club off Belvedere Road behind Tree Town; (305) 683-1711 or 428-6018. Full-production musical reviews performed along with your fine sit-down dining. Select from a twelve-item menu. Reservations required.

Trader Jack's Seafood Company   2381 Palm Beach Lakes Boulevard; (305) 697-0001. Fine seafood, including clams, mussels, and bluepoint oysters. Also steaks and veal.

Sala Del Toro Restaurant   1415 West 45th Street (at Palm Beach Jai Alai); (305) 844-2444. Enjoy a fine dinner while enjoying the excitement of jai alai. Menu includes seafood and prime rib.

Promenade   1601 Belvedere Road (at the Royce Hotel); (305) 689-6400. Serving breakfast, lunch, and dinner. Try the Friday night seafood buffet.

The Paddock Dining Room   Palm Beach Kennel Club, 1111 North Congress Avenue; (305) 683-2222. One of the world's finest racetrack restaurants. A fine menu and an elegant atmosphere.

Margarita y Amigas   2030 Palm Beach Lakes Boulevard; (305) 684-7788. A great variety of Mexican cuisine.

La Famiglia   235 Worth Avenue; (305) 655-5959. Delicious Italian food with Vegas-style entertainment. Reservations suggested.

Speakeasy Food & Spirits   104 Clematis and Flagler Drive on the Intracoastal; (305) 833-EASY. This waterfront restaurant overlooks Palm Beach and offers fresh seafood and a raw bar. Sunday brunch. Live jazz and reggae nightly.

Heart of Palm Beach   160 Royal Palm; (305) 655-5600. Half a block from the ocean, with fine dining and a casual atmosphere. Shorts and sport shirts are OK.

The Colony Hotel   Hammon Avenue; (305) 655-5430. Continental cuisine enjoyed in an atmosphere of a private club. Also good for celebrity watching.

The Crabpot   386 East Blue Heron, Riviera Beach; (305) 844-CRAB. Live Maine lobster, stuffed fish of the day, frog legs, and a wonderful waterfront location.

Rodney's Café   420 U.S. 1, North Palm Beach; (305) 848-3131. Varied menu. Open for lunch and dinner. Entertainment in lounge. Reservations suggested.

Gen Don Restaurant and Champagne Club   1225 U.S. 1, Loggerhead Plaza, Juno Beach; (305) 627-1700. Northern Italian cuisine, including pastas, fettuccine, and fresh fish.

The Mandarin   230 U.S. 1, North Palm Beach; (305) 845-2700. Cantonese and Szechuan cooking. Reservations suggested.

ATTRACTIONS   First, a word about the relationship between Palm Beach and West Palm Beach. Palm Beach was developed almost single-handedly by Henry Flagler (1830–1913), a founder of Standard Oil Company with John D. Rockefeller. Flagler was an early version of Thurston J. Howell III.

Palm Beach was to be the most exclusive of exclusive enclaves for Flagler and his megarich chums. And so it was. West Palm Beach came into being when Flagler realized that the servants, maids, butlers, lackeys, and other peons who catered so fastidiously to the Monied needed a place to live. God knows, they couldn't actually *live* in Palm Beach. So West Palm became the world's richest ghetto.

Today, Palm Beach retains all of its blue bloodedness (well, most of it) and its snootiness . . . which is its attraction for tourists and visitors. Meanwhile, West Palm Beach took on some character of its own. Today, the town is home of the Professional Golf Association, an excellent museum of science, an art gallery, and other attractions.

Palm Beach Polo and Country Club   13198 Forest Hill Boulevard, West Palm Beach; (305) 793-1440. Some of the best polo in the world is played here. Even Prince Charles has galloped over the grounds. Tickets range from $5 to $20. Dressing down is OK, with shorts, sport shirts, and other casual attire acceptable. You can buy food here or even have a picnic from the tailgate as your car sits parked along the polo field.

Palm Beach Kennel Club   Belvedere Road and Congress Avenue (right across from the Palm Beach International Airport); (305) 683-2222.

A MINOR PROBLEM

The trend for big league ball clubs is to have one spring training facility—a complex, really—where the 40-man roster and the entire minor league system can train together. The logistical and organizational reasons for this trend are obvious. But one of the factors that makes this possible is the shrinking of the minor leagues.

Years ago, a club's minor league organization was three or four times what it is today. Teams would be fielded on levels from AAA all the way down to C and D ball. It was not unusual for a team to have 600 or 700 players in its minor league system. Today, a club might have 200.

And with the reduced minor league numbers came a reduced coaching staff.

The argument has been made, and it's a valid one, that major league clubs should have more people working throughout the season at the minor league level. A big-league team will have 4 or more full-time coaches, while the team's AAA or AA affiliates will have just a manager and a coach. Many times that second coach is part-time, a roving hitting or pitching instructor assigned not to one team but to the entire organization.

The minor league experience is a time of growth where an athlete should have all the coaching he needs, especially in the area of fundamentals. By the time he gets to the big leagues, a player should know how to play. That's not always the case.

Tracing it back even further, kids today play far less baseball than they used to ten, fifteen, or more years ago. You don't see youngsters going out to the playground and playing pickup ball just for fun. Now, they seem to play organized ball exclusively and show up to play only when a coach calls a practice or if there's a scheduled game.

The biggest difference years ago was that, by playing so much on their own, kids had a tendency to learn the fundamentals of the game, almost by instinct. They played a lot more. So in some cases today, you find players getting into the low minors with a great need for basic coaching, without the number of coaches being sufficient to the task.

Enjoy greyhound racing, gourmet dining, and casual socializing at this fine track.

Norton Gallery of Art   1451 South Olive Avenue, West Palm Beach; (305) 832-5194. More than 120,000 visitors a year take in the exhibits. Collections include French (especially late nineteenth- and early twentieth-century artists), American (O'Keefe, Hopper, Marin, and more), Chinese, and sculpture. Admission is free.

The Henry Morrison Flagler Mansion   In Palm Beach. From U.S. 1, if you're driving north, turn right on Okeechobee Boulevard, cross over the bridge to Palm Beach on Royal Palm Way. Make a left at the first traffic light and drive north a half mile on Coconut Row to the museum parking lot on the left. This mansion was built by Flagler in 1901 for his wife. Heirs sold it in 1925, and the building served as a luxury hotel until 1959. It was opened to the public as a museum in 1960. All rooms have been restored to their original beauty. Call (305) 655-2833.

Hibel Museum of Art   150 Royal Palm Poinciana Plaza, Palm Beach; (305) 833-6870. An impressive collection of art; free to the public.

The South Florida Science Museum   4801 Dreher Trail North, West Palm Beach; (305) 832-1988. Exhibits highlight paleontology, biology, oceanography, and herpetology. There are also film programs and lectures.

Lion Country Safari   Southern Boulevard West (SR 80), fifteen miles from West Palm Beach; (305) 793-1084. Enjoy roaming in more than 500 acres of animals, rides, games, and other diversions. Opens at 9:30 A.M. daily, with the last car admitted at 4:30 P.M. Maybe the biggest kick is driving past wild animals as they meander right beside your car. Of course, keep the doors locked and the windows closed.

Needless to say, some of the most interesting shopping can be found in the boutiques and shops of the Palm Beaches. Here are four of the larger shopping malls:

Boca Mall   On U.S. 1 between Second and Sixth streets, Boca Raton.

The Crystal Tree   1201 U.S. 1, North Palm Beach.

Garden Square Shoppes   PGA Boulevard at Military Trail (just west of I-95 in Palm Beach Gardens).

Oakbrook Square Courtyard Shops   Corner of PGA Boulevard and U.S. 1, North Palm Beach.

Other activities include the beaches (just drive along the coast and pick out one you like), theater, golf, tennis, boating, and fishing.

For more information, contact:
West Palm Beach Chamber of Commerce
501 North Flagler Drive
P.O. Box 2931
West Palm Beach 33401
(305) 833-3711

BEFORE YOU GO

So the lure of horsehide and spring sun becomes too irresistible, and you decide to pack the family up for your Florida vacation. Here is some useful information to help you on your trip.

PLANNING The most important rule to follow is to plan early. Earlier than you think is necessary. Florida in March is an extremely popular destination, and things fill up fast. The busiest of the busy weeks of spring training are college spring break and Easter.

Book plane, car rental, and hotel reservations at the same time. Remember to ask your hotel if it offers transportation to popular attractions. Some do. Another thing to look into is a package plan. Some hotels offer plans that include discount tickets to attractions as well as deals on car rentals and even on room rates if you stay a certain amount of time. Check with your travel agent or call the hotel customer service staff.

PACKING The Coleman-Valenti Law of Packing states that you never need as much as you think you'll need. Be reasonable (and ruthless, if you have to be) about deciding what to pack and what to leave behind. Some general guidelines follow.

Bring long pants, a few long-sleeved shirts, and closed shoes, such as running shoes. Spring Florida nights, and even some days, can be windy and cool. Plus, all the buildings are air-conditioned. Don't forget sunscreen, sunglasses, and a hat or visor. The sun can be brutal if you're not prepared for it.

Put heavy items (shoes, jackets, alarm clock) on the bottom of your suitcase so they don't wrinkle your other clothes. On top of that, put the easily wrinkled items: shirts, pants, skirts. The top layer should consist of things you'll want to use, or need, right away, such as nightclothes, toiletries, and so on.

JUST BEFORE YOU GO Make arrangements for the driveway to be shoveled out (or lawn mowed, depending on where you live). Ask a neighbor to pick up your mail; leave your house key with someone you trust and have them check your property every few days. Put your valuables in a safe, hidden place or in a safety deposit box.

Another good idea is to put your lights and a radio on a timer. Empty your refrigerator and lower the thermostat. If you have an answering machine, don't say how long you'll be gone. Keep the usual greeting on it, but check frequently for messages.

Check with the police to let them know you're going away. They may have additional tips for you.

PETS It's best to leave pets at home. But if you must take a pet along, be sure to check with your hotel or motel to see if pets are welcome. Bring your pet's innoculation records. By the way, it's against Florida law to leave a pet unattended in a closed car, even briefly. Under the Florida sun, inside temperatures of a parked car can reach 160 degrees Fahrenheit in a few minutes, even with the windows partially open.

PLAYING IT SAFE Leave valuables at home. If you do bring them, lock them in the hotel safe. Otherwise, management is not responsible for loss or theft. Carry traveler's checks instead of cash. Have a record of all your credit card numbers. Keep suitcases locked in the trunk of the car and not on seats, where they can tempt thieves. Always keep your hotel room locked when you're not there, even when you leave for the briefest periods, such as getting ice.

TANNING TIPS Respect the sun. It can be murder. The most lethal sun is over open salt water; the reflected rays will burn through even the deepest tan. While boating or fishing—anywhere near reflective water—use a sunscreen lotion (the higher the number, the more protection), wear a hat and shirt, put extra cream on your nose, and keep your lips greased up with lip balm.

When you're inland poolside, you won't burn as fast . . . but you will burn if you're unprotected. Again: keep protected, until you build a good foundation.

Here's a schedule that can help take you safely from pallor to tan. Again, be sure to use sunscreen:

Day one and two: ten minutes on each side
Day three: fifteen minutes on each side
Day four: twenty minutes on each side
Day five: thirty minutes on each side

This should give you a good foundation for longer exposures, though you should never do more than an hour at a time on each side. Hour after hour of sun exposure will age your skin and greatly increase the chances of cancer.

AIR TRAVEL Book your flight early. Do some shopping to get the best possible rate. Air fare to Florida is the most competitive in the country, and if you take the time to compare, you'll save yourself a bundle. When you find the flight you want, pay for your tickets immediately, if possible. This guarantees the rate, even if the price goes up later.

Florida has thirty-two airports. The major ones are located in Tampa, Miami, Orlando, Ft. Lauderdale/Hollywood, and Jacksonville.

TRAIN AND BUS Amtrak offers service to Florida, with stations in Clearwater, Delray Beach, Deerfield Beach, Ft. Lauderdale, Jacksonville, Kissimmee, Lakeland, Miami, Ocala, Orlando, St. Petersburg, Sanford, Sebring, Tampa, West Palm Beach, Winter Haven, and Winter Park. If you want to take your car down on the train, call Amtrak for Auto Train information at 1-800-424-1111.

Greyhound and Trailways serve Florida. Seats in the middle offer the smoothest ride. That can be important on a long trip. Some bus stations can be problem areas, so be alert when going in or out of the station.

CAR Allow yourself at least a couple of days to get to Florida by car if your journey is more than 500 miles. Have the car thoroughly checked and in top shape before you begin your drive. Breaking down far away from home is one of life's biggest hassles. Go through the following checklist:
• driver's license
• insurance card
• gasoline credit cards
• registration
• set of extra car keys

- maps
- flashlight, extra batteries, flares
- first-aid kit
- properly inflated spare tire

There are six state "welcome centers" for car travelers. They are at I-95 near Yulee, at Tallahassee, U.S. 1 and 301 at Hilliard, I-10 at Pensacola, U.S. 231 at Campbellton, and I-75 close to Jennings.

RESTAURANTS We've listed restaurants for each spring training city earlier in the book. Now, a few things in general. Florida's specialty, of course, is seafood. Be on the lookout, however, for some restaurants trying to palm off the frozen variety on you and calling it fresh. If it's fresh, the restaurant will usually make a point of saying so, using the word "fresh." If you're not sure if it's fresh, don't be afraid to ask.

Fresh Florida fish specialties include stone crab, mullet, shrimp, oysters, pompano, catfish, spotted sea trout, crawfish, and grouper.

If meat's your thing, you're in luck, too. Florida is in the top ten of the country's cattle production. The best beef raising (and usually eating) is in the central part of the state.

For tips, leave 15 percent of the total bill. If the service is exceptionally good or bad, vary the amount accordingly. Reward excellent service with 20 percent. While we're on the subject of tipping, hotel porters should get 50 to 75 cents per bag.

Eating out is expensive. You can save a few dollars by having some meals in a cafeteria-style restaurant, such as Morrison's, a chain in several cities. In the better restaurants, lunch is usually less expensive than dinner. Picnics and other do-it-yourself meals can also bring down the food bill.

INFORMATION The chambers of commerce listed in the book for each spring training town are the best places for specific area information. Here are few more general resources:

Bureau of Visitor Services
Florida Dept. of Commerce
Tallahassee 32301
(904) 488-7300

Florida Dept. of Natural Resources
Division of Recreation and Parks
M.S. Douglas Building
3900 Commonwealth Boulevard
Tallahassee 32303
(904) 488-7326

Florida Division of Tourism
Visitor Inquiry Section
Dept. GM
126 Van Buren Street
Tallahassee 32301
(904) 488-5606

Florida Trail Association
Box 13706
Gainesville 32604
(904) 378-8823

There . . . you are an expert. Well, as much of an expert as you need to be to really have a great time with baseball and Florida. Oh, by the way, if anyone asks you, Florida has over 30,000 lakes, 1711 streams, and 1000 keys (or small islands, only 62 of which are inhabited). Now you are even armed with trivia. Have a blast!

PART III

Tracin'
SCORECARDS

HOW TO KEEP SCORE

The following pages contain blank scorecards you can use when you go to spring training games.

Scoring a game is fun; it also keeps you in the game and involved with the action.

Keeping score is like running for president or making love: there's no single correct way to do it. Each person has his or her different style. The most important thing about keeping score is this: develop a system that works for you and stick with it.

Scoring can be as simple as it needs to be or as complicated as it has to be. Writers and broadcasters have to keep score in such a way that they can account for each batter and runner, each base he moves to, defensive alignments, and sometimes, each pitch. If a batter is called out on strikes as opposed to swinging, that will be recorded with an extra symbol. Walks and strikeouts will be recorded in different colors so they stand out easily. They go into such detail obviously because, as part of their jobs, they have to recount games to their readers and audiences.

Fortunately, you don't have to be so precise . . . which makes scoring easy.

There's a numbering system for scoring a baseball game that goes this way:

Each defensive player has a number; not the number on the back of his uniform, but a number assigned to his position for scoring purposes. These are:

> Pitcher — 1
> Catcher — 2
> First baseman — 3
> Second baseman — 4
> Third baseman — 5
> Shortstop — 6
> Left fielder — 7
> Center fielder — 8
> Right fielder — 9

When you hear the P.A. announcer give the lineups, you write the players' names with their corresponding position numbers.

For example, if Steve Sax is the leadoff man playing second base, you write in the first position on the Dodger lineup card: "Steve Sax, 4" and so on. You record outs by using the defensive player's number. If Sax flies out to the right fielder, you simply put "9" in the box. If the next batter grounds to the shortstop, you would put in the box "6-3."

When a batter gets a base hit, you may simply want to put one short horizontal line in the box (a double is two lines, a triple three lines, and a home run four lines, or the abbreviation "HR"). Or you could simply write out the word "single."

Here are some commonly used symbols for different plays:

Fielder's choice: FC
Reaches on an error: E
Sacrifice: SAC
Stolen base: SB
Hit by pitcher: HBP
Wild pitch: WP
Force out: FO
Passed ball: PB
Balk: BK
Strikeout: K
Walk: BB

A slightly more sophisticated method for scoring uses each block in the scorecard as a miniature diamond. Home plate is the lower left corner, first base the lower right corner. Second base is the upper right corner, and third is the upper left. A player's progress around the bases is recorded on the "diamond" of the scorecard.

In the example below, the batter singled, stole second, went to third on a wild pitch, and scored on a sacrifice fly to the right fielder. Notice that the run is circled. This makes it easier to pick up the runs when glancing at the card.

To repeat, the key to good scoring is to find a comfortable system. The theme song for scoring is definitely "I Did It My Way."

Once you find that system, stick with it, so that scoring becomes automatic. After all, the more you have to think about what to do when you're scoring a game, the less you'll actually watch the game. While you're struggling with your notation, the next batter could come up and do something.

One other point to mention. Generally, it's best to score a game in pencil. Invariably, entries will have to be changed, either as a result of your error or because of a change in scoring. Pencil will allow you to erase (keep an eraser handy, of course). You might use a pen to highlight certain plays, such as strikeouts or runs scored.

On the following pages, you'll find some blank scorecards to use during grapefruit league play.

Date of Game   _____

Place   _____

Team Name   _____

BATTER	1	2	3	4	5	6	7	8	9	10	AB	R	H

Teams _____ vs. _____

Starting Pitchers _____ vs. _____

Relief Pitchers _____ vs. _____

_____ vs. _____

_____ vs. _____

Team Name _____

BATTER	1	2	3	4	5	6	7	8	9	10	AB	R	H

Date of Game   _____

Place   _____

Team Name   _____

BATTER	1	2	3	4	5	6	7	8	9	10	AB	R	H

Teams   _____ vs. _____

Starting Pitchers   _____ vs. _____

Relief Pitchers   _____ vs. _____

                        _____ vs. _____

                        _____ vs. _____

Team Name   _____

BATTER	1	2	3	4	5	6	7	8	9	10	AB	R	H

Date of Game _____

Place _____

Team Name _____

BATTER	1	2	3	4	5	6	7	8	9	10	AB	R	H

Teams _____ vs. _____

Starting Pitchers _____ vs. _____

Relief Pitchers _____ vs. _____

_____ vs. _____

_____ vs. _____

Team Name _____

BATTER	1	2	3	4	5	6	7	8	9	10	AB	R	H

GAME NOTES AND AUTOGRAPHS